The Ultimate Guide to Successful Leadership Job Interviewing

M. L. Miller

Published by SoaringME Publishing

ISBN-13: 978-1-956874-14-3

CONTENTS

Preface

Dear Reader,

As a recruiter, I have been placing frontline managers since 1998, mid-level managers since 2000, and have been working exclusively with Executive Level candidates since 2009. My journey to writing this book began in 1997 when I sought out a recruiting firm to find a job, but instead, ended up working for the firm's owner, Larry. Through my work with Larry, I gained invaluable experience in recruiting, and interviewing.

Over the years, I have had the privilege of recruiting for a wide range of roles and working with organizations of all sizes. Through this experience, I have gained valuable insights into the hiring process and what makes a successful candidate. When I began to focus exclusively on executive recruiting in 2009, I continued to receive requests for help from candidates who were just starting out. This inspired me to start my company SoaringME, where I help candidates improve their interviewing skills and succeed in their career goals.

After years of reflecting on my experiences and the lessons I have learned, I have finally put pen to paper to share my knowledge about successful interviewing. The advice I offer in this book is based on decades of experience and covers everything about interviewing to land your dream job or promotion.

This book includes all the information from my other book *SoaringME The Ultimate Guide to Successful Job Interviewing*, with additional content specifically geared towards excelling in interviews for leadership positions. Whether you're a seasoned professional or just starting out, my hope is that this book will provide you with valuable insights and tools to help you succeed in your career.

Best of luck, and I hope that you get the job or promotion that you're going for!

M. L. Miller

Founder, SoaringME

If you enjoy this book, please give it a review.

Visit

SoaringME.com

for additional resources.

Introduction

Welcome to *SoaringME The Ultimate Guide to Successful Leadership Job Interviewing,* where I offer you insights and advice on how to increase your chances of success in any job interview process. With over two decades of experience in talent acquisition that began in 1997, I've accumulated a wealth of information that, when read thoroughly, will help you land your dream job.

For employers, the hiring process is an investment in time and resources, so companies have developed a series of interviews and assessments to find the best candidate. This process is designed to uncover information about you that the employer needs to determine whether you're the best match for the job and the organization. The interview questions are created to test your knowledge, skills, and behavior to evaluate whether you align with the company's values, vision, and goals.

Interviews can be stressful, especially when you're not familiar with the process, resulting in anxiety and missed opportunities. However, the best-prepared candidates maximize their chances of success by understanding the employer's expectations, researching the company, and developing a plan to respond to common interview questions. These candidates demonstrate confidence and provide clear and concise answers that align with the job's requirements.

In this book, I offer you advice on how to prepare for an interview, what to expect, and what employers are looking for. You will learn how to demonstrate your value and how to make an informed decision about whether the job is right for you. I'll also teach you what questions to ask employers, and what employer red flags to watch out for.

Even if you are a seasoned professional with a lot of experience, it's essential to understand that interviewing is a skill that requires practice and preparation. This book will help you gain the confidence and skills needed to ace your next job interview. With the information and advice provided in this guide, you'll be able to navigate any interview process with ease, reduce your anxiety, and maximize your chances of landing your dream job.

Leadership Careers

A rewarding career in leadership encompasses a variety of stages and opportunities for personal and professional growth. Exceptional leaders exhibit essential qualities such as innovative thinking, a clear vision for their team, a passion for their work, and the ability to build, mentor, and effectively communicate with their team members. These individuals possess a strong sense of self, are active listeners, demonstrate emotional intelligence, adapt to changing circumstances, and take responsibility for their decisions. Ultimately, the best leaders view their roles as a commitment and a duty, rather than merely being in charge.

The journey of a leadership career often starts with securing a first-time frontline management position. At this stage, one acquires foundational leadership skills, such as guiding a team, setting goals, and making decisions. As an experienced frontline manager, you will have the opportunity to manage a small team and make a direct impact on the business.

As your experience and skillset expand, you may aspire to mid-level management roles, where you can lead larger teams and make strategic decisions that influence the company's overall direction. This stage offers the opportunity to further develop your leadership capabilities and gain a broader understanding of the organization's inner workings.

The transition into senior and executive-level management requires a unique combination of strong leadership, strategic thinking, and comprehensive industry knowledge. In these roles, you are responsible for developing and implementing a vision for the company, while also leading the execution of that vision to drive growth and success.

Ultimately, reaching the C-suite or serving on a board of directors necessitates a wealth of experience, a proven track record of success, and the ability to drive business growth. Top-level management demands not only outstanding leadership skills but also a deep understanding of finance, strategy, and the capacity to make difficult decisions in the best interest of the company and its stakeholders.

A career in leadership offers a multitude of pathways and opportunities for growth, advancement, and personal satisfaction. It requires hard work, dedication, and a passion for leading teams and driving business success. As you progress through the various stages of leadership, you'll find that each new challenge provides opportunities for learning, self-improvement, and making a meaningful impact on the organization and its people. By embracing these opportunities and consistently striving to enhance your leadership abilities, you can make a lasting and positive impact on the lives of those you lead and the organizations you serve.

Throughout your leadership journey, you'll encounter diverse experiences, from mentoring new team members to navigating complex business challenges. As you face these situations, you'll develop a strong network of professional relationships that will serve as an invaluable resource throughout your career.

As a leader, you'll also discover the intrinsic rewards of empowering others to reach their full potential, fostering a culture of collaboration and continuous improvement, and contributing to the overall success and growth of the organization. The personal satisfaction that comes from inspiring and motivating others, making a difference in their lives, and seeing the tangible results of your leadership efforts is immeasurable.

In a leadership career, the importance of self-reflection and continuous learning cannot be overstated. As you advance, you'll encounter new challenges, opportunities, and perspectives that will require you to adapt and grow. Embracing this ongoing process of self-improvement is vital for reaching your full potential as a leader.

Ultimately, a career in leadership is both rewarding and challenging, offering countless opportunities for personal growth, professional development, and meaningful impact. By remaining committed to your own development and the success of those you lead, you can leave a lasting legacy and make a real difference in the world of business.

Understanding What Recruiters and Hiring Managers are Looking For

To succeed in any interview process, it is vital to have a comprehensive understanding of what the interviewers are seeking. The foundation of this success lies in spending ample time to grasp as much detail as possible about the ideal profile being sought.

When a company decides to create a new job, it's because they have a need in their organization, and if they find the right person, the company will be more successful. To identify the ideal candidate, companies start with outlining the duties required for the role and develop a profile of the best-suited employee. Depending on the organization's size, the hiring manager, Human Resources, Talent Acquisition, upper management, or a combination of these may create this profile. The profile can be influenced by the hiring manager's personal preferences, the team's current makeup, or the previous employee's qualities.

The ideal candidate's profile comprises hard skills, soft skills, and personality traits, and while these traits vary slightly from company to company, most employers seek some specific traits in a new employee. These traits might not even be mentioned in the job advertisement, but interviewers still evaluate candidates on them. In the chapter on *How to Stand Out from Others*, we cover how understanding these hidden traits can provide an edge over other candidates.

Here are the eleven most common universal traits that interviewers are seeking.

1. Effective communication skills.
2. Passion for that work.
3. Self-motivated.
4. Works well with others.
5. Competent.
6. Ability to take responsibility for work and mistakes.
7. Good problem-solving skills.
8. Honest.
9. Ability to listen.

10. Nice to work with.

11. Reliable.

To identify the perfect candidate for a job, companies typically have a list of desired qualities and attributes, including educational background, training, experience, and personality traits. These may consist of a college degree, specific major, certifications, industry experience, knowledge of relevant software programs or programming languages, and other tools required for the role. The ideal candidate's personality may be characterized by being coachable, drive for future advancement, good teamwork skills, or ability to work independently.

The interview process is a series of steps designed to assess how well a candidate matches this ideal person, with the goal of eliminating candidates who are not a good fit. The job advertisement, interview questions, and final decision on who to offer the job to are all based on this profile.

Understanding the profile for a job is critical to success, as every company has a preconceived notion of the person they want to hire. This profile can be divided into two sides: the skills or experience side and the personality or compatibility with the company culture side. By having a solid grasp of this profile, you can position yourself as the best-suited candidate and increase your chances of securing the job.

Here are the best steps to understanding the ideal profile for a specific job.

1.   Research 10-20 job ads for similar jobs. Make a list of the duties required and desired attributes listed in all these advertisements.

2.   Research the backgrounds of employees who are currently in similar roles. Look at the 10-20 LinkedIn profiles and the background they had before being hired for a job like the one you want.

3.   Ask contacts in your professional network what they think makes people successful in that job, or if they know what type of candidate that company prefers to hire for that type of role.

4.   Compile the attributes that repeatedly show up in your research. This is a great starting point for understanding what the interviewers are going to evaluate you against.

To succeed in an interview, it's crucial to understand the list of required and desired attributes listed in the job advertisement. These traits are usually listed in descending order of importance, and understanding them is crucial to your success. The *COMPANION WORKBOOK The Ultimate Guide to Successful Job Interviewing* includes exercises that can help you understand the job profile, which may include many unwritten desired traits that you'll need to research.

It's important to note that job profiles usually represent a wish list for the hiring manager, not an absolute minimum. If you match 60% or more of the job profile, you should apply for the job. Some managers may take a chance on a candidate who only possesses 60-70% of the desired skills if they fit the ideal personality and are trainable on the rest. However, it's unlikely that you'll receive job offers in most cases where you're only a 60-70% match, and you may not even be interviewed.

During the interview, make sure to highlight areas in your background that relate to the job profile and avoid providing irrelevant information. Your resume should show the overlap you have with the ideal profile, and you should provide more detailed answers during the interview. For example, a nurse or therapist job profile may include experience working with elderly patients, so you should highlight your experience in this area.

Understanding the ideal profile is essential, as demonstrated by a Vice President candidate I worked with who didn't advance after the first interview. Despite having the necessary education and skillset, the candidate displayed hesitation in making decisions and asking questions during the interview with the startup employer. The role called for an individual who could take charge, be assertive, and propel projects forward. This candidate's prior experience with large corporations, where they functioned as a mere cog in the wheel, was a better fit for their personality which did not align with the desired personality traits. It's crucial to note that comprehending the ideal profile does not imply pretending to be someone else, but rather showcasing how you meet the requirements through your conduct and responses during the interview process.

Leadership Profile

Effective leadership is an essential quality for all levels of management. Whether a frontline, mid-level, or executive-level manager, the ability to inspire, motivate, and guide a team towards achieving their goals is crucial. To be an effective leader, one must possess a unique set of skills, including innovation, vision, passion, and the ability to build and coach a team. Persuasive communication, self-awareness, active listening, and emotional intelligence are also essential attributes that a leader must possess.

Frontline managers, who are responsible for the day-to-day operations of their team, must have excellent communication and problem-solving skills. They should have 2-5+ years of progressive experience in the same or similar field or 1-3+ years of previous frontline management. They must be able to handle multiple tasks simultaneously and have a strong understanding of industry regulations and standards. Additionally, they should have a bachelor's degree in a relevant field or equivalent work experience.

Mid-level managers usually must have a bachelor's degree or higher in business, management, or a related field. They should have 5+ years of experience in managing teams, preferably in the same industry. They must possess a demonstrated success record in managing teams and achieving business goals, strong leadership and communication skills, and an ability to develop and implement strategic plans. Also, they should have a proven track record of making sound decisions and solving problems effectively, experience with budget management and financial analysis, excellent interpersonal skills, and the ability to build strong relationships with internal and external stakeholders. Furthermore, they should have the ability to work effectively in a fast-paced environment and adapt to changing circumstances, proficiency in relevant software and technology related to the industry, and a willingness to travel as needed.

At the executive-level, management roles require exceptional communication and leadership skills, a deep understanding of finance, strategy, and business operations, and the ability to make difficult decisions in a fast-paced environment. Executives typically must possess at least a bachelor's degree in a related field, and they should have at least ten years of industry related experience. They must have a proven track record of driving business growth and achieving strategic goals, strong analytical and problem-solving abilities, and experience managing large teams.

Successful executives should be able to navigate complex business environments, stay ahead of industry trends, and make tough decisions that ensure the long-term success of the company. They must have the ability to build strong relationships with stakeholders, develop and implement strategic plans that lead to significant rewards, both professionally and financially. Moreover, they must possess a deep commitment to the job, have a strong sense of self, be highly adaptable and resilient, and understand that leadership is not just about being in charge and telling others what to do.

Effective leadership is a fundamental requirement for all levels of management. Each level of management offers unique opportunities for growth and advancement, and managers play a vital role in shaping the lives and careers of their team members. They are responsible for providing guidance, support, and training, as well as setting clear expectations and goals for their employees. With the right skills, mindset, and dedication, anyone can achieve success in this field.

How You Will be Evaluated

Preparation is essential for a successful interview. Candidates who don't prepare are viewed as less professional and less interested, leading to fears of underperformance and short tenures if hired. The most successful candidates plan, understand the employer's ideal profile, organize their thoughts and memories, and relate their skills, experience, and traits to that profile.

Employers use the ideal profile to develop an interview process that evaluates candidates' suitability for the position. Interviewers may be experienced enough to ask individual questions, while others may use an interview packet. To understand what interviewers are seeking in your answers, imagine yourself as the interviewer looking for the ideal profile.

For example, imagine you're interviewing candidates for the Director or Senior Director of Regulatory Affairs role in a biotech company. Apply this same process to whatever job you're interviewing for to prepare for a successful interview.

Here is part of the job advertisement that explains the ideal profile that we're looking for:

Primary responsibilities include:

- Participates with key stakeholders to formulate regulatory strategies.
- Plan and manage integration of multidisciplinary regulatory programs into the project team development plans for all assigned projects.
- Lead the planning of and conduct meetings with regulatory agencies as appropriate. May represent the company at regulatory agency meetings as appropriate.
- Perform regulatory intelligence activities to keep current on the regulatory environment and competitive products.
- Provide the company with current and proposed regulatory and scientific issues.
- Manage and review safety reports and submissions.

Education and Skills Requirements:

- Demonstrated knowledge of the drug development process is essential.
- Knowledge of laws and regulations affecting the pharmaceutical industry and regulatory experience.
- Must have prior experience working with the FDA or EMA.
- Experience in successful NDA, BLA or MAA filings is essential.
- Prior management experience preferred. Must demonstrate the ability to work through others.
- Highly organized, with attention to detail.
- Advanced scientific degree preferred. B.A. or B.S. or higher degree(s) in the sciences, or health-related field minimum, with 7+ years of regulatory experience (Director) and 10+ years of regulatory experience (Sr. Director.) Demonstrates personal leadership and collaboration skills.
- Travel up to 25%.

To prepare for an interview, imagine yourself as one of the interviewers. I will provide you with an interview packet that contains a list of traits we are looking for in the ideal candidate and ten to twenty different questions for each trait. These questions are designed to assess the candidate's skills or experience and evaluate their proficiency in that area.

For instance, the packet for the Director or Senior Director of Regulatory Affairs role in a biotech company might include traits like regulatory strategy, leadership, communication skills, and attention to detail. Under each trait, the packet will provide questions that will help evaluate the candidate's abilities and how they fit the ideal profile.

By practicing this mental exercise, you can anticipate the type of questions that interviewers may ask and prepare accordingly. This way, you'll be better equipped to demonstrate how you match the ideal profile during the interview and improve your chances of success.

"Prior management experience preferred. Must demonstrate the ability to work through others." As you prepare to interview these candidates, here is how your packet questions might look for the management experience that we are looking for:

Management experience:

Q1: How do you give feedback to others, and how do you hold them accountable?

Q2: Tell me about a project that you led. What made it successful?

Q3: How do you manage stress among team members?

Q3: Tell me about a time that you influenced other team members on a project. How did that work out?

Q4: Describe to me a time when you managed somebody who was struggling.

Q5: How do you plan for your team members' professional development?

Q6: How do you handle conflict between team members?

Q7: Tell me about a time when you had to let a team member go. Why? How did they take it?

Q8: How do you motivate people?

Q9: How have you successfully delegated to others?

Q10: What is your biggest management weakness?

During the interview process, each interviewer will usually be assigned three to five traits to evaluate in the candidate. The interview packet contains a list of ten to twenty questions for each trait, and each interviewer will choose one question to ask the candidate. There may be some overlap where multiple interviewers evaluate the same skill, and the candidate's resume may affect the questions asked.

In addition to hard skills, interviewers are also evaluating personality fit and how long it will take the candidate to become a highly contributing member of the team. After all interviews are completed, interviewers will compare candidates in a feedback meeting and may develop a favorite candidate to advocate for. Candidates who create multiple advocates will have a higher chance of getting the job offer.

To succeed in the interview process, prepare well for each interview, regardless of the interviewer. Get into a relaxed, professional, and likable frame of mind to make a good impression. By doing so, you can create advocates and increase your chances of securing the job.

This is how your answers are analyzed.

As a candidate, every answer you give in an interview must meet the minimum credibility standard set by each interviewer. For example, taking credit for territory rankings or success in a sales position after just three months may not be credible if the typical sales cycle is six to nine months. Similarly, claiming to be downsized when your former company is hiring and expanding will also harm your credibility. Only credible answers will increase the strength of your candidacy.

Interviewers prioritize the strength of a candidate's answers when evaluating feedback and making hiring decisions. A strong answer leaves the interviewer with confidence that you could be a good employee, and the strength of your answer is directly related to the impression you leave with the interviewer. The hierarchy of impressiveness may vary depending on the type of interview questions and the industry or sector of the job.

Therefore, when preparing for an interview, pay special attention to how impressive your answers are likely to be. This will help you organize your thoughts and memories in a way that highlights your strengths and presents you as a strong candidate.

Hierarchy of impressiveness for interview answers.

1. Verifiable accomplishments. (i.e., awards, recognition, publications, or rankings.)
2. Accomplishments that are harder to verify.
3. Good success stories that directly relate to the job.
4. A good example of past success that indirectly relates to the job.
5. An example that demonstrates a personality trait that fits the profile.
6. Demonstrating personality traits during interviews.
7. Hypothetical answers describing what you would do in a future situation.
8. Showing related work experience. (Higher rank if successful during that experience.)
9. Opinion: self-descriptive statements trying to convince the interviewer how   great you are.
10. Answering with a lot of words but avoiding the actual question that was asked.

11. Awkward silence.

12. Lying.

Although companies do not have a formal hierarchy list, interviewers often rank candidates' answers based on a hierarchy of impressiveness. For example, if you are interviewing for a job in the commercial industry, your strongest answers should demonstrate how you made or saved money for your previous employers. While it's important to convey your strongest highlights, avoid memorizing verbatim answers.

To make a strong impression on the interviewer, focus on highlighting your accomplishments and results in previous roles. Be prepared to provide specific examples of how you contributed to the success of your previous employers, especially in areas that are relevant to the job you are interviewing for. By showcasing your ability to make a positive impact on the company's bottom line, you can demonstrate your value as a potential employee.

How we assess candidate potential.

Employers seek candidates who have the potential to grow and improve while performing well in their current role. During the interview process, interviewers evaluate certain traits to assess a candidate's potential for growth and development. I have used the following list as my guidance in the past to determine candidate potential:

- **Motivation**

High-potential candidates possess a strong drive to excel and achieve significant accomplishments, but their goals extend beyond their individual success. They also strive for collective objectives and demonstrate humility, investing time and effort to improve their skills and abilities in all areas. This dedication to both personal and collective growth sets them apart as exceptional candidates.

- **Curiosity**

Candidates who possess a desire for personal growth tend to have a natural inclination towards exploring new experiences, seeking knowledge, and receiving honest feedback. These individuals remain open to learning and embracing change, recognizing that personal development is a continual process that requires dedication and an eagerness to expand their horizons.

- **Insight**

The capacity to gather and interpret data in a way that reveals fresh perspectives and opportunities is a valuable trait that sets candidates apart. Being able to discern patterns and connect seemingly unrelated information helps in identifying new possibilities and finding innovative solutions. This ability to gather and make sense of information is a critical skill for success in many industries.

- **Engagement**

Being able to communicate a compelling vision effectively is a highly sought-after skill by employers. Those who possess a talent for using both emotion and logic to persuade others are especially valuable. The ability to connect with people on an emotional level, while also using logic to present a clear and persuasive message, is essential for successful communication. This skill can help build strong relationships, motivate teams, and drive the achievement of shared goals.

- **Determination**

The perseverance to pursue challenging objectives in the face of obstacles and the resilience to recover from setbacks. Hiring determined candidates can bring a sense of motivation and drive to the workplace, which can inspire others to work harder and achieve more. Determination is often an indicator of a candidate's passion for their work and their commitment to producing high-quality results. This quality can also help employers identify individuals who are likely to persevere through challenges and contribute to the company's success.

Understanding the perceptions that interviewers likely have.

Interviewers may ask questions based on your resume or as a follow-up to one of your answers. Understanding how others perceive your background is key to highlighting your strengths and mitigating shortcomings. For instance, having a strong track record with a well-respected company is an advantage.

Startups often prefer candidates with experience in both established and small companies. Large organizations are known for providing comprehensive training, which can be beneficial for a candidate's next job. However, startups have a different culture, and hiring managers may prefer candidates who have previous experience in an entrepreneurial environment to ensure that they understand the culture and are a good fit.

Academic credentials from renowned institutions, such as Harvard or Stanford, can be beneficial, but they do not guarantee success. Candidates who project arrogance due to their education may not make a good impression. It is important to be self-aware and demonstrate eagerness and capability to learn.

Candidates with a history of short-term employment may be viewed with suspicion, as it may suggest issues with skills or personality. During the interview process, it is crucial to uncover any history of inferior performance or conflict with management/co-workers.

Getting some extra help – Understanding the recruiters.

When you are going through an interview process, you might work with a recruiter, either an inside/corporate recruiter or an outside/third-party recruiter, commonly referred to as a "Headhunter" for executive-level roles. Regardless of the type of recruiter you work with, there are some basic commonalities to their job, the most important being that if you impress them, they often become your advocate.

Corporate Talent Acquisition Recruiters are given goals for the number of hires they need to fill at their company, with their job performance evaluated by the metric of "Time-to-Fill". Quality-of-Hire is also tracked in many companies, including retention, performance, and promotion of employees hired by that recruiter. If you can impress the recruiter, they can become an advocate to get you hired, as it reflects well on their job performance.

Outside recruiters, including headhunters, have a direct financial incentive to become advocates for strong candidates. Most are paid on a contingency basis, meaning they only receive payment if they fill the position. If you impress an outside recruiter, they will become an advocate for you, potentially introducing you to opportunities at multiple companies.

Understanding the incentives of recruiters will help you take advantage of their assistance, and building long-term professional relationships with good recruiters can benefit your career. However, it's important to be mindful of your actions, as behaving inappropriately can damage relationships. For example, directly contacting a hiring manager without informing your recruiter can lead to negative consequences and harm your chances of future opportunities.

How to Answer Behavioral-Based Interview Questions

Behavioral-based interview questions are based on the premise that past behavior is the best predictor of future behavior in similar situations. These questions are also known as competency-based, behavioral, situational-based, or performance-based interviews. There is a related style of questioning called skill-based interview questions. To succeed in these types of interviews, it's important to prepare in advance.

Situational-based interview questions are hypothetical, but the strongest answers are those that draw from actual experiences in comparable situations. To increase your chances of success, there is a simple exercise you can do before the interview. But before we get into that, let's cover some common advice for answering these types of questions.

Behavioral interviews are designed to test your ability to work well in various scenarios, including high-pressure situations, tight deadlines, and urgent needs. The interviewer wants to see if your decisions and attitude align with the qualities they're seeking in a candidate. You'll likely be asked to provide specific examples of times when you've been in similar situations.

To answer behavioral questions effectively, take some time to reflect on your past experiences and think about which ones are most relevant to each question. This will help you stay organized and confident during the interview. When answering, be sure to give a specific example and focus on the relevant details. Avoid providing unnecessary information that may distract from your main points.

One candidate I worked with was a borderline fit for the job on paper, but her well-prepared answers to my behavioral questions set her apart from all the other candidates. Her responses were exactly what we were looking for and she delivered them with confidence and detail. Even though the hiring manager wasn't impressed by her resume, she sailed through the rest of the process and got the job. If you want to interview successfully, follow her lead, and prepare strong examples that demonstrate the qualities the interviewer is seeking.

What is the standard advice on how to respond to behavioral-based interview questions?

Here is a list of what you can do to prepare for behavioral interview questions:

1. Examples should be tailored to the ideal profile.

2. Make a list of your previous efforts and significant achievements.

3. Formulate your answers using the STAR technique, which I will explain in this chapter.

4. Be succinct and precise in your answers.

Examples should be tailored to the ideal profile.

During a behavioral interview, it's important to remember that the interviewer is looking for specific qualities in a candidate. Your answers should provide clues that you are a good fit for the profile they're seeking. To tailor your responses to their needs, pay attention to the job description. For instance, if the position requires three years of experience and proficiency in certain software programs, you should be prepared to talk about situations where you used those programs or similar ones. By doing so, you'll show the interviewer that you have the skills they're looking for and increase your chances of landing the job.

Make a list of your previous efforts and significant achievements.

To succeed in a behavioral interview, it's crucial to spend time preparing in advance. Make a list of projects from your career that are relevant to the job you're applying for, and if you're early in your professional life, don't hesitate to use examples from your academic career if they're applicable. During the interview, be sure to include details of your experiences that demonstrate your qualifications for the job. In particular, explain how your actions led to success for your employer. If, for example, you were responsible for a significant increase in sales, be prepared to discuss the steps you took to achieve that outcome and how you can replicate that success in the future. By organizing your experiences and highlighting your achievements, you'll be well-equipped to impress the interviewer and secure the job.

Formulate your answers using the STAR technique.

The STAR technique (situation, task, action, and result) is the most popular method for answering behavioral interview questions in a clear and thorough way. Some people may refer to it as SOAR (situation, obstacle, action, and result), but it's essentially the same thing. By using this technique, you can break down your responses into easy-to-follow components that effectively convey your experience in a previous job. Each element of STAR offers a framework for telling your story when answering behavioral-based interview questions. With this technique, you'll be well-prepared to respond to questions in a way that showcases your skills and achievements and increases your chances of landing the job. Here is an explanation of each stage and an example:

- **Situation**

Describe a situation relevant to the question asked that you have faced in your work, and any essential facts the interviewer should be aware of. Prioritize pertinent information that relates to the position you are looking for.

Consider the following scenario: *"Our team had a backlog of articles that needed to be submitted and authorized by the customer in my previous job as an internal copywriter. The editors imposed strict deadlines on us in order for us to finish the items in our queue, which caused me stress."*

- **Task**

Tell the interviewer about the responsibilities that you had in this scenario. This explains the specifics of what you needed to accomplish on behalf of your former company to reach a goal. As I will explain later in the chapter, this is the least important part of the STAR technique.

"My job was to make sure that over the following five days, I produced and submitted three articles to fulfill the fifteen-article goal set by my project manager to assist the team in catching up."

- **Action**

Explain the steps that you took to meet your deadline and accomplish the objective you set for yourself. Create a list of the top talents that you want to communicate to the interviewer for this stage, which should emphasize the skill you are attempting to convey to the interviewer.

"Over the course of this period, I set up three two-hour time slots in my schedule to work on these three articles. If I had any concerns, I called the project manager, and I shut out any other distractions by listening to classical music to maintain my concentration on writing."

- **Result**

Define the results achieved due to your activities. When feasible, provide statistics or specific quantifiable outcomes and how they impacted the business at the time. You want to give a clear timeline, completion timeline, and the impact of your decisions.

"I ended up producing and submitting eight articles at the end of the week, more than double my planned goal. As a result, we were able to meet our deadline and ended up expanding our relationships with those clients."

Be succinct and precise in your answers.

When answering behavioral interview questions, it's important to keep your responses concise, ideally under two minutes. To achieve this, consider practicing with a mentor or friend who can help you focus on the main points while keeping your answers brief. Alternatively, record yourself answering the questions and listen back to assess the length and quality of your answers. Keep in mind that the interviewer may shift gears and ask different questions, so be prepared to adapt accordingly. By preparing in advance and delivering concise, relevant responses, you'll make a strong impression and increase your chances of landing the job.

Examples of Behavioral-based interview questions:

1. Describe the most challenging situation you have had to deal with in the last year.

2. Describe a moment when you exceeded your manager's expectations to help a customer.

3. Tell us about a time when a colleague needed motivation and what you did to help them.

4. Tell us about a time when your workload was a problem. What steps did you take to address this problem?

5. Have you ever felt pressured to meet a deadline? What methods did you use to deal with this problem?

6. Describe a time when you committed a blunder that had a negative impact on your team. How did you deal with that situation?

7. Tell me about a time that you had to rapidly pick up a new skill. What was the outcome, and how did you go about learning your new skill?

8. Tell me about when you had to pitch an idea to upper management. What was the outcome?

9. Have you ever had a disagreement with a coworker about the project's direction? What did you do to come to a compromise with your coworker?

Using the STAR method, here is an example of a successful behavioral-based interview answer:

Describe the most challenging situation you have had to deal with in the past year.

"I received a call from a client a year ago regarding a complaint he had about the software we provided. He stated that he wanted to cancel his account with us because the software had shut down while he was working on a critical project for his company. I asked him to take me through what had happened step by step so that I could better understand what had happened."

"After hearing his story, I decided that we should offer to refund the money he had paid for the month that the problem occurred. I called my manager and explained the situation to get her approval. Then I worked with one of our engineers to figure out the technical problem the client

had with our software. I was able to refund him the money and fix the issues with his software at no additional charge. This action resulted in retaining the account, and the consistent payments from a top client, contributing to a profit increase for my company."

This answer is successful because it takes the interviewer through a success story where you are the star of that story, and your company benefited by having you as their employee. It mostly follows the STAR method but illustrates why I am telling you that there is a more effective, and efficient method to prepare for a behavioral-based interview.

The best way to prepare to successfully answer behavioral-based interview questions.

1. Start with one or more blank sheets of paper and turn them horizontally to be in a landscape layout. (Of course, you can do this digitally if you prefer.)
2. Draw two vertical lines down the page so that you create three equal columns.
3. At the top of the left column write "Situation", center column "Action", and on the right "Results".

4. Re-read the ideal profile you wrote or the job advertisement, the duties, requirements, and any other parts that describe what the company is looking for in the person that they hire.

5. Using only bullet points, start listing specific examples from your career that relate to the ideal profile.

6. After you have put as many relevant examples as you can recall, set this page aside and when you remember another fitting example, come back to it, and jot it down. (This might take a couple of days.)

7. Once you have all the most relevant examples, re-write your page and rank them so that your best examples are listed at the top (the ones that you don't want to leave the interview without making sure you mention them.), and then list the remainder in descending order of impressiveness.

To improve your performance in behavioral-based interviews, consider using the SAR (Situation, Action, Results) technique instead of STAR (Situation, Task, Action, Results). While tasks and responsibilities are important, they're typically less significant than the situation, action, and results of your story. Focusing on these elements will make it easier to remember a greater number of examples and their details. When answering questions, start with the situation, describe the action you took, and conclude with the results you achieved. By keeping it simple and straightforward, you'll be more productive and confident.

Preparing with the SAR exercise before your interview can help you recall examples and deliver a confident, successful answer. Taking a moment to recall your list of examples, choosing the best one for the question, and sharing your success story demonstrates confidence and impresses the interviewer. Without this preparation, candidates may struggle to recall examples from their past, leading to a less confident and less impressive performance. To access this exercise and other helpful resources, check out the **COMPANION WORKBOOK: *The Ultimate Guide to Successful Job Interviewing.***

Final behavioral-based interview insights.

Many candidates dislike behavioral-based interview questions because they believe they can make up stories to get hired. However, these types of questions are just one tool used to make hiring decisions. Experienced recruiters and hiring managers can spot inconsistencies and check on claims made in answers.

Candidates who are dishonest may save the interviewer time by demonstrating why they should not be hired.

The most common mistake candidates make when answering behavioral-based interview questions is to avoid answering them altogether. For example, if a candidate is asked for an example and responds with a vague non-answer like "I deal with that all the time..." or "I have many clients who do that...", they have failed to provide a specific example related to the question. After a few vague answers, most interviewers will eliminate the candidate from consideration.

Another mistake is not listening to the entire question. Candidates often focus on the example they want to use and stop listening to the interviewer. However, there may be multiple parts to the question, and candidates need to listen carefully to provide an appropriate answer.

To prepare for behavioral-based interview questions, write out bullet points for success stories and practice saying them aloud. Avoid memorizing verbatim answers and speak naturally during the interview. Remember that interview questions are chosen to determine if a candidate fits the ideal profile for the job. Answers should include examples of skills, temperament, experience, and talent that match what the company is looking for.

Canned, disingenuous answers are not recommended. Instead, memorize bullet points and speak naturally during the interview. Interviewers are also assessing personality fit, and coming across as fake or reciting answers can be detrimental to a candidate's success.

Quick reference summary:

1. Prepare ahead of time using the SAR exercise.
2. Do not make up examples.
3. Give real examples from your experience.
4. Listen to the entire question.
5. Practice saying your examples aloud before the interview.
6. Relate all your examples to the ideal profile.

Focus on the main points that you need to make.

How to Answer the Most Common Tough Interview Questions

Many job applicants have experienced the sinking feeling of being caught off-guard by unexpected or tough interview questions. While it's impossible to anticipate exactly what interviewers will ask, being familiar with common difficult questions, their purpose, and how to approach them can help job seekers feel more confident and ready.

Interview questions are designed to assess how well a candidate matches the ideal profile that an organization is looking for. For example, the classic "tell me about yourself" question has stumped many candidates. I have seen two types of candidates fail this question: the overconfident and the intimidated. Later in this chapter, I will provide tips on how to avoid these pitfalls.

Successful candidates typically prepare for tough interview questions in advance, taking the time to tailor answers to a specific organization or employer. This can make interviews go more smoothly and make applicants more impressive to interviewers. Some tough questions push candidates to think critically and creatively, while others catch candidates off guard.

No matter how challenging an interview may seem, getting hired depends on how prepared a candidate is relative to other applicants. The key is to demonstrate how well you match the job requirements and specifications. Your answers should be concise and relevant, connecting your experiences to the ideal profile.

Understanding the job and candidate profile can provide insights into the questions you may be asked during an interview. Successful interview preparation often involves practicing answering questions with a partner, recording and listening to your answers, and practicing until you are comfortable and confident. Avoid memorizing answers verbatim and instead focus on the main points you want to make and speak naturally.

Despite being a great fit on paper, I have interviewed thousands of job candidates who fell short in the interview. On the other hand, candidates who seemed less qualified on paper impressed me in the interview. To help you succeed, take a closer look at some of the most common difficult interview questions, and examples of how to answer them.

Interview questions that are difficult to answer and how to respond to them.

"Tell me about yourself."

Reason we ask: The interviewer is trying to evaluate how much of a match you are to what they want to hire. This question/statement is a quick way for us to gather certain information; do you understand the job and what we are looking for? Do you have the education and/or experience we want? For some jobs, we are evaluating your presentation skills.

Answering the open-ended question "Tell me about yourself" is an excellent chance to showcase how you align with what the interviewer is seeking. Many candidates make the mistake of giving long-winded, irrelevant answers that lack detail related to the job. For this reason, it is helpful to take a chronological approach, starting from when you began your career or education up to your current position. Your answer should be concise and no longer than 30-60 seconds, and it should include relevant achievements that demonstrate how you align with the job requirements.

When responding, you should address both the skills and personality traits required for the position. Avoid generic responses like "Unique" or "Hardworking" and instead, connect your experience, skills, and personality traits to what the employer is looking for in the ideal candidate.

Highlight specific areas where your background matches the job requirements, such as your education, experience with specific software programs or languages, or other skills that are relevant to the position. If you can, try to connect a personal trait to the company culture or the job description.

To make your answer stand out, add a brief statement that sets you apart from other candidates. Specifically, you should include your Unique Value Proposition (UVP). Your UVP should be a brief statement that clearly explains your skills, experience, and unique strengths in a way that appeals to this employer. Based on your research or knowledge about the company or industry, mention something about yourself that makes you more qualified for the job than most other candidates. To learn more about the UVP, please read my book *SoaringME **The Ultimate Guide to Successful Job Searching***.

Matching your skills and personality to the ideal profile is critical in creating a strong response to this question and developing compelling positioning and closing statements. Spend time crafting a concise and powerful answer that demonstrates your ability to meet the job requirements.

What to avoid: Throughout my years of conducting interviews, I have noticed two types of candidates who consistently fail when it comes to answering the questions, "Tell me about yourself", or "Why are you a good fit for this position?" The first type is the overconfident candidate who tends to use clichés and self-promoting language without providing any evidence to back up their claims. I once had a candidate repeatedly describe themselves as an "All-star" several times during an interview without offering any examples that supported this statement. Needless to say, he did not come across as convincing and did not move forward in the interview process.

The second type of candidate who often struggles with this question is the intimidated candidate. They may not see how their skills and experiences align with the position and fail to mention them in their answer. However, it is crucial to research the job and company beforehand and identify the ways in which you are a good match. Your answer should not be about bragging but about demonstrating your qualifications for the position.

Confidence is key when answering this question. Be sure to highlight your relevant experiences and skills that make you a strong fit for the position. Avoid using generic language and provide concrete examples to support your claims. Remember, it is not just about showcasing your skills and experiences, but also about demonstrating how they align with the job requirements and company culture. By preparing and delivering a strong answer, you can stand out as a top candidate for the job.

"What are your biggest weaknesses?"

Reason we ask: Your answer to this question should tell us how self-aware you are, and if you have a weakness that makes you not compatible with the job or company.

When asked about your biggest weakness, it's important to understand that the interviewer may also phrase the question as "What is something your boss has told you that you need to work on?" or "What is one thing that you would change about yourself?" The key to answering this question is sincerity. Avoid presenting a positive trait as a flaw or mentioning a personality trait, as these responses can come across as insincere. Instead, discuss an actual professional shortcoming that you have identified, worked on, improved upon, and that will not negatively impact your performance in the job you are interviewing for. This demonstrates self-awareness and a commitment to professional growth.

Example answer of a candidate interviewing for an Executive Assistant role: *"In my previous job as a Copywriter, I lacked enough creativity to consistently produce new original content. I took workshops and I got better, but I never felt like it was what I was best at. I'm good at writing and staying organized, so I decided to find a career that was a better match for my strengths."*

The creativity needed to be a Copywriter is not required to be an exceptionally good Executive Assistant. The answer displays self-awareness and the ability to improve but does not make the interviewer doubt that the candidate is a match for the role.

What to avoid: It is crucial to avoid certain responses when asked about your biggest weakness in a job interview. The worst answer would be to claim that you do not have any weaknesses. This response portrays a lack of self-awareness and raises a red flag that you might be a difficult employee. The second-worst answer is to mention a skill from the ideal profile for the job, which could be perceived as a lack of preparation and effort. Cliché responses like "I'm a workaholic" or "I can be too driven by my work" come across as insincere and should be avoided. It's important to choose an actual professional weakness that you have identified, fixed or improved, and are continuing to work on.

"Why should I hire you over somebody else?"

Reason we ask: This answer will tell the interviewer how well you understand the job, how much of a match you are to what we want to hire, and some insight into your enthusiasm.

To prepare for "Why should I hire you over somebody else?" question, focus on practicing for "Tell me about yourself" and

"What is your greatest strength?" questions. A successful answer should demonstrate your understanding of the job and the ideal candidate profile. Provide a concise overview of how your experience and skills align with the position. Show why you are the best candidate for the job and the company without comparing yourself to others. Create a compelling and succinct explanation of why your services are valuable to the business.

Example answer for a candidate interviewing for a Data Engineer role: *"I believe that my experience lines up well with what you are looking for. My experience is directly transferable, and I have strong coding skills in both Python and R. More than just being a technical fit, I am passionate about what you're doing here and would really enjoy working on the types of projects you need done."*

What to avoid: Many candidates give a rehearsed answer to this question, which can sound artificial and insincere. It's best to avoid discussing other candidates or being negative about them, as it may indicate that you have difficulties working with others.

"Why are you interested in this job?"

Reason we ask: The answer to this question gives the interviewer insights into your career goals; how much you know about this position and company, whether you did your research, what your motivation is, how strong your motivation is, what is most important to you. All of those help us determine how much of a fit you are. Applicants who simply want any job become employees that do not stay long, and this question is an attempt to screen them out of the process.

Your response to this question should showcase that you have taken the time to research the company and the position, and that you are enthusiastic about the opportunity. While it is important to connect your background to the ideal profile, the focus of your answer should be on the company itself. Identify two or three unique attributes of the company's culture, history, products, or reputation that differentiate it from other employers. Your response should demonstrate that you are motivated, professional, and have a genuine interest in the company and the position.

Example answer:

"I'm extremely impressed with this PQRS Therapeutics reputation, and I think that your science might be the next big breakthrough. My PhD was focused on immunology, and for the past five years I have been working with Immuno-Oncology cell therapies. I think you are on the

right path with what you're developing, and I would love to be a part of advancing this type of science."

What to avoid: Mentioning compensation or benefits and displaying a lack of enthusiasm in your tone or body language are two mistakes to avoid when answering this question. Focusing too much on salary and perks can give the impression that you are not passionate about the job or the company, but only interested in what you can get out of it. Similarly, a disinterested tone or negative body language can give the impression that you are not fully invested in the opportunity, which can be a turn-off for the interviewer.

"What is your biggest achievement?"

Reason we ask: The answer to this question should give the interviewer insight into both your skills and your personality. When you choose what you consider to be your biggest achievement, it gives us insight into what you consider to be most important. Understanding what your priorities are in the workplace will help us determine if you are a good fit for our company culture. We also need a certain level of skill in the people that we hire, so understanding what you did and how well you did it for your biggest achievement will inform us about your skill-level.

Many people struggle with answering this question because they are not used to promoting themselves. However, it is a vital opportunity to showcase your accomplishments and how they align with the job you are interviewing for. Your answer should not only demonstrate an achievement but also how it could positively impact the company or team, whether it is through boosting sales or improving collaboration. Depending on the job requirements, you may also highlight your personal achievements if they show that you are a good fit. Practicing your answer beforehand can help you feel more at ease with selling yourself during the interview.

Example: The startup software company is hiring an outside sales representative. A competitive nature is a must have trait. They would prefer previous experience, but it is not required.

Answer 1: *"When I began in my current position the company had not even launched its first software program. It was a challenging start, but I built relationships with key decision makers within our target market* and ended up winning sales representative of the year out of our team of twenty."

Answer 2: *"I am highly driven and results-oriented, but since this will be my first professional job after graduating, I'd have to say that my greatest achievement to-date has been that I was named captain of my college soccer team three years in a row. I love what I know about your software, and I look forward to being a top performer for you, like I was in my athletic career."*

What to avoid: Do not give a vague response and instead, use a specific achievement. It's essential to be honest and avoid taking undue credit for something that was not solely your accomplishment. If you were part of a team, make sure to explain your significant contribution to the success. This answer should be backed by specific examples and not be merely a general statement. Be prepared for follow-up questions that may scrutinize your individual role in the achievement.

"What would your co-workers say about you?"

Reason we ask: Being self-aware is a particularly important soft skill for most organizations. Understanding how your behavior is perceived by others allows you to get along better with co-workers and to be more productive. Your answer to this question should give us an idea of how self-aware you are, and about your personality. We will compare your answer to all other evidence we have or observe about you. We want to see if you would be a good fit for the company culture and this question helps us make that determination.

Before the interview, take time to evaluate your own strengths and skills, and then compare them to the ideal profile that the company is seeking. Make a list of anecdotes from your work that showcase these skills. When answering this question, highlight one or at most two of your strengths that align with the job requirements. Start by telling the interviewer about these strengths and then back them up with examples from your experience.

Example answer: *"In my current role as a data engineer, most of my co-workers would describe me as a creative problem-solver. Just last quarter my team and I encountered an integration problem that we couldn't find an existing solution for. After analyzing a couple of work-around options, I presented my ideas to the team, and we worked together to solve the issues."*

This answer demonstrates both that the candidate is a creative problem-solver, but also that he/she works well within a team.

What to avoid: It's crucial to be honest while answering the interview questions. You should never fabricate skills or give false examples. The interviewers may cross-check some of your responses with others who have interviewed you. Making up skills or experiences that you do not possess is not only unprofessional but also a surefire way to lose the opportunity. **Being dishonest is the fastest and most sure-fire way to guarantee that you don't get the job.**

"What are your biggest strengths?"

Reason why we ask: This is a straightforward way for us to assess what you are best at and if that matches what we wish to hire. Your answer may also give us further insight into your personality, such as determining if you are self-aware and our view of a good fit.

The employer schedules an interview with you because they are interested in learning more about the qualities that you possess. Always keep in mind that there are other applicants competing with you for the job. It is advantageous to highlight a skill that sets you apart from other applicants, or that you excel in.

Notable strengths do not necessarily have to be hard skills; some employers are looking for the right personality that can be trained. Therefore, behavioral qualities such as tenacity or resilience might be essential when analyzing the ideal profile for the job.

When describing your greatest strength, it is important to provide evidence that supports your claim. You should give an example of a time when you displayed this strength and how it produced a positive result. A strong example that demonstrates your skill is crucial to make your answer stand out from other candidates. Lastly, your answer should tie back to the job you are interviewing for. You can simply add a brief statement at the end of your answer that explains how this strength will contribute to your success in the position.

Follow these steps to prepare for this question:

1. Make a list of your biggest strengths, experience, education, training, hard and soft skills.
2. Self-assess and rank the skills on your list or the order in which they are your strongest attributes.

3. Make a list of the desired qualities based on your understanding of the ideal profile.

4. Start with the first listed attribute that the company desires, and if it is listed as one of your top strengths, this should be the focus of your answer. If not, go to the second listed attribute on the company list. Continue until you find a genuine strength of yours that is highest on both lists.

If you can't find an overlap between the job requirements and your strengths, but you believe that one of your strengths will be valuable in this position, you must tailor your response to emphasize how this skill is relevant to the job. It's okay if you have two strengths to highlight, but keep your answer brief, lasting no more than two minutes.

Example answer: *"I have excellent organizational skills. While I was going to college full-time, I also worked twenty hours a week in the accounting department at XYZ Corp. At that job my primary responsibility was consolidation of overseas quarterly financial reports, and my boss never had to make an adjustment to any of my work. I was able to complete my accounting degree on time and graduated with honors. I know my ability to organize my time and complete projects accurately will help me be successful in this role."*

The impression this answer gives is that not only is this candidate organized, but also smart, hard-working, and motivated.

What to avoid: The way you answer this question can reveal a lot about your character and suitability for the job. Overconfidence may suggest that you are not open to constructive criticism and unwilling to improve. Conversely, being too modest may lead the interviewer to question your self-assurance and ability to excel in the role. The key is to strike a balance between confidence and humility, demonstrating that you are self-aware and coachable. Choose a strength that is specific and relevant to the job, avoiding generic or overly common answers.

"Why are you leaving your current job?" / "Why did you leave your previous job?"

Reason we ask: This question does inform us about your motivation, and whether this career move makes enough sense to lead us to believe that you will be a long-term employee for us. But the tricky part of this question is how much we can learn about your personality.

Complaining about your current or previous job, colleagues, or bosses during an interview can leave a negative impression on potential employers, even if your complaints are genuine. Instead, focus on what you want to achieve in your next career step and match those desires with what the new job offers. Always try to relate your answer back to how you are a good fit for the opportunity. The approach to answering this question might differ depending on how you left your previous employment. Therefore, I am providing some scenarios and example answers to guide you.

Example answer for someone who voluntarily left/are leaving on good terms with their employer:

"I am grateful for the opportunity that I had at ABC Company, it was a wonderful experience but it's just time for me to take on a new challenge and show that I can accomplish even more than I already have. Your company will provide me with the opportunity to do that."

Example answer for someone who voluntarily left/are leaving on less than good terms with their employer:

"I learned a lot in my time with ABC Company, but over time I realized what I really need is an opportunity that is going to both challenge me and allow me to work with a product that I can be passionate about. I really like what I've learned about your company and products. This is a better fit for me and where I want to take my career."

Example answers for someone who was laid-off by their employer not due to performance:

"Unfortunately, my company went through a re-structuring in April. Since I was one of the most recent hires, I was part of a group that was let go. I have received an above average performance review, and my manager will be one of my references. The work that I had done well in that position is very similar to your position so I'm confident I will get up to speed very quickly."

Example answer for someone who was terminated by their employer:

"When I was originally hired it was because they were looking to bring a different skill set into ABC Company. I made appropriate changes and we did increase sales by 33%, but it quickly became clear that the President and I have different styles. I learned that to thrive, I need an innovative and collaborative environment, which is exactly what I see that your company promotes itself to be."

Notice that this answer is not negative towards the previous employer or boss, makes the point that at least some of the work done was good, and brings it all back to being a good fit for this new job. It does not give every detail about being fired and does not tell a lie. You should expect follow-up questions about some of the details, but continue to be concise, honest, positive, and professional. If you made a mistake at your previous job, explain how you have learned from it and why it will not be a problem for your next employer.

What to avoid: It is not appropriate to share negative experiences or personal conflicts with previous employers during an interview. Over-explaining or becoming emotional about your reasons for leaving a previous job should be avoided as well. Honesty is important, but it is never acceptable to lie about how you left a previous job. Remember that background checks are typically conducted, and if dishonesty is discovered, it could lead to termination from the new job.

"What are your salary expectations?"
(See the later chapter entitled *The Job Offer.*)

M. L. Miller

Successfully Answer Technical Interview Questions

Technical interviews are designed to evaluate a candidate's skill level in a specific area that is essential for success in a technical job. This type of interview is commonly used in industries such as tech, engineering, and finance/accounting. The questions asked will vary depending on the specific technology or skill being evaluated and can differ from one interviewer to the next. In this chapter, I provide an overview of what to expect in a technical interview.

To prepare for a technical interview, there are several online resources available that provide up-to-date questions that are being asked at specific companies. While the questions asked may vary from one interviewer to the next, preparing for commonly asked questions can help you feel more confident and increase your chances of success. It is also recommended that you not only research technical interview questions at the company you are applying to, but also their competitors, to prepare more thoroughly.

It is important to note that technical interviews are designed to screen for skills, and it is crucial that you have a solid understanding of the specific technology or skill being evaluated. By doing your research and practicing your skills, you can approach a technical interview with confidence and increase your chances of landing the job.

You can expect technical interview questions to cover these areas.

1. Your experience. (Including behavioral-based questions focused on the technical aspects of the job.)
2. Brainteaser questions to test your applied thinking.
3. White boarding. While the actual whiteboard has been going out of style as of late, there will be some variation in coding interviews to evaluate your current skills.

During a technical interview, it is not just your technical skills that are evaluated. The interviewer is also looking to assess your personality and soft skills. If you are being considered for a team-oriented position, communication is a critical skill that the interviewer will be evaluating. Solving a problem is one thing, but being able to communicate your thought process and ideas is equally important. A successful employee is someone who can work collaboratively with others to achieve a common goal. Thus, candidates who engage in a back-and-forth conversation with the interviewer while discussing their problem-solving process tend to be more successful in interviews.

Also, intellectual curiosity and passion for technology are far too overlooked in technical interviews. **Companies are much more likely to hire a person with passion who can be coached-up on their hard skills, than an expert who lacks enthusiasm for their work.**

Questions about experience can be direct questions about what you have worked on, or like the questions I covered in the chapter on *How to answer behavioral-based interview questions.*

Examples of technical interview behavioral-based questions.

"Tell me about a project you worked on that failed."

And *"Tell me about the most challenging tech problem you have faced in the past couple of years. How did you solve it?"*

What are we looking for? You have the ability to overcome challenges and work well within a team.

"Tell me about a tech project that you have worked on in your spare time."

What are we looking for? Your passion.

"Tell me about a time where you were asked to do something that you had never done before. How did you go about it?"

What are we looking for? Ability to work independently, and your self-motivation.

Examples of technical interview direct questions.

"What online resources do you use to help you do your job?"

What are we looking for? Your passion, resourcefulness, and ingenuity.

"How do you keep your technical skills current?"

What are we looking for? Your passion and professionalism.

"Pretend I'm not a tech person; how would you explain 'X' to me?"

('X' represents the technology used in this job or your past job.) What are we looking for? Your communication skills, especially if the job will require you to explain things to less technical people. And, to a lesser extent, gives some insight into your technical knowledge.

Technical interviews are renowned for their unorthodox and abstract questions. The purpose of such interview questions is to assess your thought process and how well you can reason your way through a problem. The emphasis is not on providing the correct answer to an insignificant question. We are looking for individuals who can think quickly and support their responses with a sound explanation. Thus, it is crucial to communicate your logic effectively during the interview process. While solving a problem, it is best to articulate your thought process in real-time. Even if you take a wrong turn, it is acceptable to explain how you recognized your error and found a better approach.

Examples of these curveball questions:

"How many golf balls would it take to fill an SUV?"

"A scientist puts a bacterium in a Petri dish at noon. Every minute, the bacteria divide into two. At exactly 1 p.m. the Petri dish is full. At what time was the dish half full?"

"Describe the internet to someone who woke up from a 30-year coma."

As I recommended earlier, do your research on what companies in your industry are currently using.

Many companies use challenging scenarios or problems to evaluate your expertise in the job role. These questions are designed to test your problem-solving abilities and how well you can apply your knowledge and skills to real-world situations. It is important to remain calm and focused during these technical interviews and answer the questions to the best of your abilities. Don't be afraid to ask for clarification or additional information if needed. Remember, the interviewer is not necessarily looking for the correct answer but wants to see how you approach the problem and your ability to think critically and creatively.

Here are suggestions to prepare for this part of the technical interview:

1. Study for technical interviews through current books, websites, and online videos to learn the latest questions you are likely to be asked.

2. Study the technology used at the company and the position.

3. Focus on refreshing the basic knowledge for that technology.

If you are unsure about the technology or the question, it is best to clarify and admit that you do not have the answer but try to demonstrate your knowledge of related technologies. Technical interviews are not just about getting the right answer but also about showcasing your thought process and problem-solving skills. To prepare for these interviews, it is important to have a strong foundation in relevant areas and demonstrate your ability to approach a problem from a high-level perspective. Avoid getting sidetracked by minor details and stay focused on the main issue at hand.

Common Interview Questions for
Leadership Positions

When conducting interviews for leadership positions, I prefer to start with open-ended questions to assess a candidate's communication skills, ability to prioritize information, and persuasiveness in their responses. Alongside these open-ended questions, I also include specific queries aimed at determining the candidate's relevant experience and gauging their boldness, innovation, vision, passion, coaching and team-building skills, self-awareness, listening ability, adaptability, emotional intelligence, and willingness to take responsibility. By using a mix of open-ended and targeted questions, I can gather a comprehensive understanding of the candidate's leadership potential.

In addition to assessing a candidate's skills and experience, I aim to create a comfortable environment where the candidate feels encouraged to share their ideas, opinions, and experiences with me. This approach allows me to evaluate whether the candidate has the necessary personality traits to excel in a leadership role within the organization.

Below are common interview questions for different levels of leadership roles. There may be some overlap as we are trying to uncover common traits at each level.

Common interview questions for first time managers.

"What would your priorities be in your first 90 days if you get this job?"

Reason we ask: This question aims to understand your priorities, planning abilities, understanding of the role, and your sophistication as a leader.

As a first-time manager candidate, it's crucial to have a well-structured plan for your first 90 days in the role. When asked about your priorities, avoid providing a generic answer. Instead, tailor your response to the specific job you're interviewing for. Start by highlighting the key areas you plan to focus on, such as building relationships with your team members, recruiting to fill any open roles, getting to know the organization's culture, and understanding the team's goals and objectives.

Example answer (for a candidate interviewing for a Sales Manager role): "If I were to be hired for the Sales Manager role, my top priorities in the first 90 days would be to meet with each team member individually to understand their strengths, opportunities for improvement, and what motivates them. Additionally, I would prioritize getting to know the sales team's current sales processes and identify areas for optimization and improvement. Finally, I would work on building strong relationships with the rest of the leadership team to understand their priorities and align the sales team's goals with the organization's objectives."

What to avoid: Avoid giving a vague answer that does not demonstrate a clear understanding of the role or responsibilities. Avoid over-promising and committing to unrealistic goals that you cannot deliver. Additionally, avoid being overly focused on individual goals and not considering the team's objectives. It's essential to strike a balance between personal and team goals. Lastly, do not forget to mention your willingness to learn and be open to feedback to show your commitment to growth and development.

"Can you give an example of how you have developed and mentored team members in the past?"

Reason we ask: This question aims to understand your ability to develop and mentor your team, which is a critical skill for any managerial position.

As a first-time manager candidate, it's important to have prior experience in developing and mentoring team members. When answering this question, highlight a specific example of how you mentored a team member and helped them achieve their goals.

Start by outlining the team member's strengths and areas for improvement, then discuss the steps you took to support them, such as providing regular feedback, coaching them on specific skills, and setting achievable goals.

Example answer (for a candidate interviewing for a Customer Service Manager role): "In my previous role as a Team Leader, I had a team member who was struggling with handling difficult customers. I recognized her strengths in other areas and identified that her lack of confidence was the root cause of the problem. I worked with her to provide additional training and support to improve her confidence, which helped her handle difficult customers with ease. Additionally, I provided regular feedback and coaching to help her develop her skills, which resulted in a 20% increase in customer satisfaction scores for her team."

What to avoid: Avoid providing a generic answer that does not demonstrate a clear understanding of the skills required for mentoring and developing team members. Avoid mentioning a situation where you did not successfully mentor someone or one where you made a significant mistake that impacted the team member negatively. Instead, focus on a specific example where you were successful in mentoring and developing a team member. Lastly, do not take full credit for the team member's success, as it could come across as arrogant. It's essential to highlight the team members' hard work and dedication as well.

"Can you tell us about your previous experience?"

Reason we ask: This is an open-ended question that aims to uncover how much of a match you are to the ideal profile for the role you're interviewing for.

As a first-time manager candidate, it's important to demonstrate how your previous experience has equipped you with the necessary skills and knowledge for the new role. When answering this question, focus on specific examples of how your previous experience is relevant to the new position. Start by highlighting the key responsibilities and achievements in your previous roles and how they relate to the current role. Emphasize how you have gained relevant skills such as leadership, problem-solving, communication, and project management.

Example answer (for a candidate interviewing for a Project Manager role): "In my previous role as a Project Coordinator, I was responsible for overseeing the project's timelines, budgets, and ensuring the team's deliverables were met. I gained extensive experience in managing cross-functional teams, coordinating with stakeholders, and communicating project progress. Additionally, I was able to successfully lead the team to deliver a project on time and within budget, which resulted in a 10% increase in customer satisfaction scores."

What to avoid: Avoid mentioning irrelevant experience or responsibilities that do not relate to the job. Also, avoid exaggerating your achievements, as it could come across as dishonest. Instead, focus on providing specific examples and evidence of how your previous experience has equipped you with the necessary skills and knowledge for the new role.

"How do you handle situations where you need to motivate and manage individuals with different personalities and work styles?"

Reason we ask: This question aims to understand your strengths and opportunities when managing and motivating individuals, which is a critical skill for any managerial position.

As a first-time manager candidate, it's essential to have experience in managing and motivating individuals with different personalities and work styles. When answering this question, highlight a specific example of how you managed a team with diverse personalities and work styles. Start by outlining the different personalities and work styles you encountered and the challenges you faced. Then, discuss the steps you took to understand each team member's needs, such as providing individual coaching, setting clear expectations, and acknowledging each team member's contributions.

Example answer (for a candidate interviewing for a Sales Manager role): "In my previous role as a Sales Representative, I had a team of individuals with diverse personalities and work styles. Some team members were more introverted and preferred to work independently, while others were more extroverted and enjoyed working collaboratively. To be an effective leader on the team, I made an effort to understand each team member's communication style, motivation, and career goals. I provided individual coaching, communicated the expectations of our management team, and recognized each team member's contributions. This approach helped me to effectively lead the team and exceed our sales targets."

What to avoid: Avoid exaggerating your abilities or claiming that you can handle any situation, as it could come across as unrealistic. Instead, focus on providing specific examples of how you mentored a diverse team and how you overcame the challenges you faced. Lastly, do not forget to highlight your willingness to learn and be open to feedback, as it shows your commitment to growth and development.

"Can you tell us about a time when you had to make a difficult decision as a team leader?"

Reason we ask: This question aims to assess your decision-making skills and how you handle difficult situations, which are critical skills for any managerial position.

As a first-time manager candidate, it's essential to have experience in making difficult decisions as a team leader. When answering this question, provide a specific example of a difficult decision you had to make, the factors you considered, and how you arrived at a resolution. Highlight how you built a consensus with your team members in the decision-making process and how you managed any conflicts or disagreements that arose.

Example answer (for a candidate interviewing for an Operations Manager role): "In my previous role as a Team Lead, we had a situation where we needed to terminate an employee who was consistently underperforming. It was a difficult decision to make, as the individual had been with the company for a long time and was well-liked by their colleagues. To ensure that we were making the right decision, we conducted a thorough performance review, and we involved the HR team in the process. We also made sure to communicate the decision clearly to the team and addressed any concerns or questions that they had. Although it was a challenging decision to make, it ultimately resulted in an improvement in the team's overall performance."

What to avoid: Avoid exaggerating your abilities or taking full credit for the decision, as it could come across as unrealistic. Instead, focus on providing a balanced and honest account of the situation and highlighting the role your team members played in the decision-making process. Lastly, do not forget to highlight your willingness to learn from the situation and how you will apply the lessons learned to future situations.

"Can you give an example of how you have effectively delegated tasks in the past?"

Reason we ask: As a frontline manager, delegation is a critical skill that helps ensure tasks are completed efficiently and effectively. This question helps us understand your delegation skills, communication skills, and your ability to lead and motivate your team.

Example answer: "As a team leader in my previous role as a customer service representative, I was responsible for managing the team's daily tasks. One of my team members was particularly strong in handling customer complaints, so I delegated this responsibility to them. I communicated the expectations and provided the necessary resources and support for them to succeed. I also checked in regularly and provided feedback to ensure that they were meeting the expectations. This delegation allowed me to focus on other critical tasks, while the team member gained confidence and developed their skills in handling customer complaints."

This answer demonstrates the candidate's ability to identify team member strengths, communicate effectively, provide necessary resources and support, and trust in their team's abilities to achieve successful results.

What to avoid: Avoid giving an example where delegation was not successful, as this may come across as a weakness in your leadership skills. Also, avoid taking credit for your team's achievements, and instead focus on how your delegation and leadership contributed to the success. Make sure that the example demonstrates increased efficiency and/or team member development, avoid an answer that may come across as avoiding duties that should not have been delegated. Lastly, avoid delegating tasks without providing necessary resources, support, and clear communication, as this may lead to confusion and failure to meet the goals.

Questions for experienced frontline managers.

"How do you motivate and inspire your team to achieve their best work?"

Reason we ask: Your answer will help us understand your leadership style, people management skills, and how you create a positive work environment for your team.

When asked about motivating and inspiring your team, it's important to highlight your leadership approach and the strategies you use to encourage your team to excel. A great answer would demonstrate your ability to understand and connect with your team, as well as your commitment to their growth and development.

Example answer: "I believe that a motivated and engaged team is key to achieving great results. I prioritize communication, active listening, and empathy to build strong relationships with my team members. I take the time to understand their individual strengths and motivations, and work with them to set meaningful goals that align with the team's objectives.

I also create a supportive work environment that encourages collaboration, creativity, and innovation. I value feedback and ensure that each team member's contributions are recognized and appreciated. Additionally, I provide my team with opportunities for learning and development through training, mentorship, and exposure to new projects. By doing so, I have seen my team become more invested in their work and more committed to achieving great results."

The answer showcases the candidate's leadership style, emphasizing the importance of communication, collaboration, and recognition. It also demonstrates their commitment to their team's growth and development, and highlights their ability to create a positive work environment that fosters creativity and innovation. I would typically ask a follow-up question after that answer to learn more details about one or more of the steps that this candidate outlined.

What to avoid: Avoid presenting yourself as a micromanager or someone who motivates through fear or intimidation. Also, avoid claiming that you don't need to motivate your team because they should be self-motivated. These responses can give the impression that you lack the skills necessary to lead and manage a team effectively. It's important to demonstrate a genuine understanding of your team's needs and to present specific strategies that you have implemented to inspire and motivate them.

"Can you give an example of a time when you had to make a difficult decision?"

Reason we ask: This question assesses your ability to make sound decisions when faced with challenging situations and how you manage tough choices. It helps the interviewer understand your decision-making process and how you handle pressure and unexpected circumstances.

Example answer: "In my previous role, we faced a situation where we had to make a decision about whether to delay the launch of a new product or launch it with some known defects. I quickly gathered information from my team and other stakeholders, including customer feedback and market trends, to help me assess the situation. After weighing the pros and cons of each option, I decided to delay the launch and work with the team to address the defects. We communicated this decision to our customers, and I made sure to be transparent about the reasons for the delay and the steps we were taking to improve the product. In the end, the decision paid off, and the product was launched successfully with no further issues."

This answer demonstrates the candidate's ability to gather and analyze data to make informed decisions, their focus on the customer, and their ability to communicate effectively with stakeholders. It also highlights their problem-solving and risk management skills.

What to avoid: Avoid using examples that could reflect negatively on your judgment or decision-making skills. Do not share a story that violates company policy or ethical standards. Also, avoid sharing an example that makes it appear that you are unable to make tough choices or manage pressure. Keep your answer focused on your decision-making process, and ensure that it demonstrates your ability to assess and manage risk while keeping the company's goals and customers in mind.

"How do you ensure that your team is meeting targets and delivering results?"

Reason we ask: This question helps us understand your management style and strategies for delivering results. It also shows us how you approach problem-solving and how you handle challenging situations as a manager.

Example answer: "As a frontline manager, I prioritize setting achievable goals with my team members that are aligned with the overall goals of the organization. I ensure that everyone is aware of their role and how it contributes to the team's success. I also emphasize the importance of regular check-ins and feedback sessions to monitor progress and identify areas for improvement. In challenging situations, I encourage my team members to provide suggestions and solutions, and I work with them to develop a plan to overcome any obstacles. I believe that collaboration and open communication are key to achieving success."

This answer shows that the candidate has a structured approach to managing teams, prioritizes goal-setting and regular feedback, encourages collaboration and open communication, and is solution-oriented.

What to avoid: Avoid giving vague or general answers that do not showcase your specific management strategies. Don't overstate your abilities or make unrealistic claims about your performance. Additionally, avoid throwing your team members under the bus or placing blame on external factors if targets are not met. Instead, focus on your solutions and problem-solving skills while demonstrating a collaborative approach.

"How do you approach performance management and development for your team members?"

Reason we ask: As a manager, it's crucial to develop and inspire your team members to achieve their highest potential. This question helps us understand your leadership style, communication skills, and ability to motivate and support your team members.

Example answer: "As a manager, I believe in setting clear expectations and goals for my team members. I regularly provide feedback on their performance, both positive and constructive, to help them improve and grow. I also encourage my team members to set personal development goals and work with them to create an actionable plan to achieve those goals. I provide the necessary resources and support, such as training and mentorship, to help them succeed. Additionally, I believe in recognizing and rewarding team members who exceed expectations and contribute to the team's success."

This answer demonstrates the candidate's approach to performance management and development, including setting clear expectations and goals, providing feedback and support, encouraging personal development, and recognizing and rewarding success.

What to avoid: Avoid taking credit for your team members' achievements, as it may undermine their hard work and dedication. Instead, focus on how you support and motivate your team to achieve their goals and exceed expectations. Finally, avoid neglecting team members who may be struggling, and instead provide the necessary support and resources to help them improve and grow.

"How do you approach setting goals and objectives for the team, and ensuring they align with the overall goals of the organization?"

Reason we ask: This question helps us understand your leadership style, communication skills, and ability to develop and execute a strategic plan that drives the team's success.

Example answer: "As a manager, I believe in setting specific and measurable goals for the team that align with the organization's overall goals and objectives. I work closely with my team members to ensure they have a clear understanding of their role and how it contributes to the team's success. I also encourage team members to set personal goals that align with their strengths and interests. I provide the necessary resources and support, such as training and mentorship, to help them achieve their goals. Additionally, I regularly review and adjust the goals as needed to ensure we are on track to meet the organization's strategic objectives."

This answer demonstrates the candidate's approach to setting clear and measurable goals, aligning them with the organization's overall strategy, providing support and resources to help the team achieve the goals, and regularly reviewing and adjusting the goals to stay on track. If there was a specific example of a team member that went through this exercise and did well, it would be an even stronger answer.

What to avoid: Avoid neglecting personal goals and interests of team members, as it may lead to decreased motivation and engagement. Instead, provide the necessary support and resources to help team members achieve their personal goals while contributing to the team's overall success. Finally, avoid setting unrealistic goals or neglecting to review and adjust the goals regularly, as it may lead to frustration and decreased motivation among the team.

"How do you ensure effective communication within the team and with other departments?"

Reason we ask: As a frontline manager, you will be responsible for leading a team and ensuring that tasks are completed efficiently and effectively. Effective communication is essential to achieving this goal. Your answer to this question should demonstrate your understanding of the importance of communication and how you prioritize it within your management style.

Example answer: "As a frontline manager, I understand the critical role that communication plays in achieving our team's goals. I prioritize communication by setting clear expectations from the outset of a project or task. I make sure to communicate these expectations to my team members and provide them with any necessary resources to succeed. Additionally, I encourage open and honest communication among team members and create an environment where everyone feels comfortable sharing their ideas and feedback. I regularly check in with my team members to ensure that they have the information and support they need to complete their tasks successfully."

This answer demonstrates the candidate's understanding of the importance of communication in achieving team goals and their commitment to creating an open and collaborative work environment.

What to avoid: Avoid responses that suggest a lack of understanding of the importance of effective communication, such as "While it isn't my strength, I do my best." or "I just tell team members what to do and expect them to follow through." Also, avoid giving vague or general answers without any concrete examples of how you prioritize communication in your management style. Finally, avoid saying that you don't have any experience in this area, as this could raise concerns about your ability to lead a team effectively.

Common interview questions for mid-level managers.

"How do you utilize analytics to improve your team's performance?"

Reason we ask: As a mid-level manager, your ability to leverage data and analytics to drive business decisions is critical for your team's success. This question provides the interviewer with insight into your experience and approach to data-driven decision-making, as well as your ability to use analytics to identify areas for improvement and drive performance.

Example answer: "In my current role, I use data analytics to regularly monitor our team's performance and identify areas for improvement. For example, I track key performance indicators such as customer satisfaction scores and sales targets to identify trends and patterns. I then work with my team to develop targeted strategies and training plans to improve our performance. I also leverage analytics to optimize our processes and workflows, identifying bottlenecks and areas where we can improve efficiency. I believe in using data to make informed decisions, but I also recognize the importance of considering qualitative feedback from team members and customers to make well-rounded decisions."

This answer demonstrates the candidate's experience and skills in using data and analytics to drive team performance and process improvements. It also highlights their ability to balance quantitative data with qualitative feedback to make well-rounded decisions.

What to avoid: Avoid overstating your skills or familiarity with analytics tools or techniques that you're not familiar with. Additionally, avoid relying solely on data to make decisions without considering other factors, such as team member feedback or customer satisfaction. Instead, focus on concrete examples of how you've used data to drive positive outcomes and improvements for your team.

"Can you give an example of how you have successfully led change initiatives within your team or organization?"

Reason we ask: Change management is a crucial skill for mid-level management candidates. Your response to this question should demonstrate your ability to lead teams through change, communicate effectively, and deliver successful outcomes.

Example answer: "At my previous job, we were facing a significant shift in our industry's market dynamics. It required us to pivot our business strategy to stay competitive. I started by gathering data and analyzing industry trends to identify areas where we needed to focus. Then, I communicated my findings to my team, outlining the need for a change in our approach. I led brainstorming sessions with the team to generate ideas for adapting to the changing market conditions. Together, we developed a new business plan that aligned with our company's overall objectives. Throughout the process, I provided regular updates and communicated the reasoning behind the change to ensure buy-in from the team. As a result of our efforts, we were able to successfully pivot our business strategy and increase revenue by 20%."

This answer demonstrates the candidate's ability to lead teams through complex changes, their strategic thinking, and their effective communication skills. It also highlights their focus on delivering successful outcomes.

What to avoid: When answering this question, avoid giving examples that don't showcase your ability to lead change effectively. Don't focus on personal achievements at the expense of highlighting the role of the team. Also, avoid mentioning unsuccessful change initiatives or ones where you faced significant resistance from team members. Finally, be careful not to take credit for the work of others or exaggerate your role in a successful change initiative.

"How do you approach mentoring and developing junior managers within your team or organization?"

Reason we ask: Your answer will help us determine your leadership style, management skills, and ability to foster a culture of growth and development.

When asked about mentoring and developing junior managers, it's important to showcase your leadership skills and highlight the strategies you use to support the growth and development of your team members. A great answer would demonstrate your ability to understand and connect with your team, identify areas for improvement, and provide meaningful guidance and support.

Example answer: "As a manager, I take pride in mentoring and developing my team members to help them achieve their full potential. I approach this by starting with a deep understanding of their skills, experience, and career goals. I make it a priority to connect with each team member, provide ongoing feedback, and help them identify opportunities for growth and development.

I believe that successful mentoring and development requires a focus on individualized development plans, where I work with each team member to create tailored learning opportunities that build on their strengths and address areas for improvement. I encourage my team members to seek out stretch assignments and new challenges to further develop their skills and gain new experiences.

I also prioritize creating a positive work environment that fosters open communication, trust, and collaboration. By doing so, I have seen my team members grow and develop in their roles, take on new responsibilities, and become strong contributors to the success of the team and organization."

The answer highlights the candidate's leadership style, emphasizing the importance of personalized development plans, ongoing feedback, and opportunities for growth and development. It also demonstrates their commitment to fostering a positive work environment and building strong relationships with their team members. If the answer also includes a specific manager as an example, it would be even stronger.

What to avoid: Avoid presenting yourself as someone who is too hands-off and doesn't provide enough guidance or support. Also, avoid focusing solely on your own achievements or accomplishments, as this can come across as self-centered. It's important to showcase your ability to understand and connect with your team, identify areas for improvement, and provide meaningful guidance and support. Additionally, avoid making unrealistic promises or setting unrealistic expectations for your team members. It's important to be honest and transparent about the support and resources that you can provide to help them achieve their goals.

(Mid-level managers should also expect more industry specific questions than frontline managers.)

Common interview questions for executive-level managers.

"Can you tell us about a time when you had to make a tough financial decision for the company?"

Reason we ask: We are interested in understanding your financial acumen and decision-making skills as an executive-level management candidate. Your answer will help us determine your ability to make tough financial decisions and guide the organization towards financial success.

When asked about a tough financial decision you made for the company, it's important to showcase your financial acumen and decision-making skills. A great answer would demonstrate your ability to analyze complex financial information, weigh different options, and make tough decisions that align with the organization's strategic goals.

Example answer: "As a CFO, I've had to make tough financial decisions that required balancing short-term needs with long-term strategic goals. One example was when our company faced a significant decline in revenue due to a global economic downturn. To address this challenge, we had to make difficult decisions regarding our workforce, including a reduction in force.

I led the development of a comprehensive financial plan that balanced cost-cutting measures with investments in growth areas that aligned with our long-term strategy. We implemented a targeted reduction in force that minimized the impact on our workforce while still achieving the necessary cost savings.

In addition to workforce changes, we implemented a series of operational efficiency measures and identified new revenue streams that allowed us to diversify our business and reduce our reliance on a single revenue source. By taking these tough decisions, we were able to stabilize our financial position, protect our workforce, and position the company for future growth."

The answer highlights the candidate's financial acumen and decision-making skills, emphasizing their ability to analyze complex financial information, weigh different options, and make tough decisions that align with the organization's strategic goals.

What to avoid: Avoid presenting yourself as someone who takes financial risks without considering the consequences. Also, avoid focusing solely on the bottom line and ignoring the impact of financial decisions on employees, customers, and other stakeholders. It's important to showcase your ability to balance short-term and long-term goals, make tough decisions that align with the organization's strategy, and communicate these decisions effectively to stakeholders. Additionally, avoid making unrealistic promises or setting unrealistic financial targets that are not achievable. It's important to be honest and transparent about the financial realities facing the organization and to develop realistic plans for achieving financial success.

"How do you measure the success of your team and individuals?"

Reason we ask: We are interested in understanding your leadership style and management approach as an executive-level management candidate. Your answer will help us determine your ability to measure the success of your team and individuals and guide them towards achieving their goals.

When asked about measuring the success of your team and individuals, it's important to showcase your leadership skills and management approach. A great answer would demonstrate your ability to set clear goals and expectations, provide ongoing feedback and coaching, and measure performance against key performance indicators.

Example answer: "As a CEO, I believe that measuring the success of my team and individuals requires a holistic approach that considers both quantitative and qualitative factors. At the start of each quarter, I work with my team to set clear goals and expectations that align with our overall strategic objectives.

Throughout the quarter, I provide ongoing feedback and coaching to each team member to help them stay on track towards achieving their goals. This includes regular one-on-one meetings, performance reviews, and informal check-ins to provide feedback and offer support.

In addition to these ongoing conversations, we use key performance indicators to measure progress towards our goals. These indicators include both quantitative measures, such as revenue growth and customer satisfaction ratings, and qualitative measures, such as employee engagement and team collaboration.

By taking this holistic approach, I am able to measure the success of my team and individuals in a way that considers both their contributions to the company's bottom line and their impact on our overall culture and team dynamic."

The answer highlights the candidate's leadership style and management approach, emphasizing their ability to set clear goals and expectations, provide ongoing feedback and coaching, and measure performance against key performance indicators.

What to avoid: Avoid presenting yourself as someone who solely focuses on quantitative measures of success and ignores the importance of qualitative factors. Also, avoid setting unrealistic goals or expectations that are not achievable. It's important to showcase your ability to set realistic goals and provide ongoing support and feedback to help your team members achieve them. Additionally, avoid measuring success solely based on individual performance and ignoring the importance of team collaboration and dynamics. It's important to take a holistic approach that considers both individual and team contributions to the company's success.

"Tell us about your vision for this role."

Reason we ask: This question helps us understand if you have a clear understanding of the job responsibilities and if you have thought about how you can contribute to the organization. It also shows your level of enthusiasm for the position and your ability to think strategically.

Example answer: "My vision for this role is to streamline our operations to make them more efficient and cost-effective. I believe that by optimizing our processes and implementing new technologies, we can reduce waste, increase productivity, and improve our bottom line. I also want to focus on talent development by investing in our employees and providing opportunities for growth and advancement within the organization. This will not only help us retain top talent but also create a culture of innovation and collaboration."

This answer demonstrates the candidate's understanding of the role and their ability to think strategically. They have a clear vision for how they can contribute to the organization and have highlighted specific areas for improvement.

What to avoid: It is important to avoid generic or vague responses when asked about your vision for the role. Avoid making it all about your personal goals and objectives or providing a generic response that could apply to any role. Additionally, avoid making promises that are unrealistic or outside of the scope of the role. Instead, focus on how you can contribute to the organization's success and be specific about the areas you plan to focus on.

"How do you prioritize and manage your time effectively?"

Reason we ask: Effective time management is critical for success in an executive-level management position, where there are multiple priorities and demands on your time. Your answer to this question should demonstrate your ability to manage your time effectively, prioritize tasks, and delegate where necessary.

As an executive-level management candidate, it's important to demonstrate your ability to manage your time effectively. When answering this question, discuss the methods you use to prioritize tasks, manage deadlines, and delegate responsibilities to your team when necessary. Talk about how you use tools such as to-do lists, calendars, and time-blocking to stay organized and on track. Mention how you make decisions about which tasks to prioritize based on their urgency, importance, and impact on the organization.

Example answer: "As an executive, I understand the importance of effective time management. I start each day by reviewing my calendar and to-do list to prioritize tasks and ensure that I'm using my time efficiently. I use time-blocking to ensure that I have dedicated time for important tasks and meetings. When prioritizing, I consider the urgency and impact of each task and delegate responsibilities to my team when necessary. I also ensure that I have regular check-ins with my team to stay informed about their progress and provide any support they need to complete their tasks on time."

What to avoid: It's important to avoid appearing disorganized or lacking in time management skills when answering this question. Avoid talking about taking on too many responsibilities or being overwhelmed by your workload. Also, avoid mentioning that you prioritize tasks based on their ease or personal interest, as this can come across as unprofessional and self-centered. Instead, focus on demonstrating your ability to manage your time effectively, prioritize tasks, and delegate responsibilities to your team when necessary.

"Please tell us about your leadership style."

Reason we ask: This question aims to understand the candidate's leadership approach and how they interact with their team. It can also give insight into their ability to delegate, provide guidance and mentorship, and inspire and motivate their team to achieve goals.

Example answer: "My leadership style is collaborative and supportive. I believe in empowering my team members to make decisions and take ownership of their work while providing guidance and resources when needed. I prioritize open communication and actively seek feedback from team members to ensure that we are all aligned and moving in the same direction. Additionally, I make it a priority to recognize and celebrate individual and team achievements to foster a positive and motivated work environment."

This answer highlights the candidate's collaborative and empowering leadership style while emphasizing the importance of open communication and recognition of individual and team achievements.

What to avoid: It's important to avoid providing a generic or vague answer that does not demonstrate a clear leadership approach. Responses that suggest a micromanaging style, lack of delegation, or an authoritarian approach may raise concerns about the candidate's ability to effectively manage a team. Additionally, it's crucial to avoid disparaging comments about past colleagues or teams as this may indicate a lack of professionalism and the potential for conflict in the workplace.

"Can you walk us through your approach to budgeting and financial management?"

Reason we ask: As an executive-level management candidate, your role will involve making important financial decisions for the company. This question allows us to understand your experience and strategies for budgeting and financial management, as well as your ability to communicate complex financial information.

Example answer: "My approach to budgeting and financial management involves three main steps. First, I analyze historical data and current market trends to develop a realistic budget. Second, I regularly review the budget and adjust it as necessary to account for unexpected expenses or changes in the market. Finally, I communicate the budget to relevant stakeholders and work with them to ensure that the budget is being followed and that any issues are addressed in a timely manner. I have found that this approach allows for flexibility while still ensuring that the company stays within its financial means."

This answer demonstrates a clear understanding of the budgeting and financial management process, as well as the ability to communicate effectively with stakeholders.

What to avoid: When answering this question, it's important to avoid oversimplifying the budgeting process or making unrealistic promises. Avoid providing vague answers that do not demonstrate a clear understanding of financial management, such as "I just make sure we stay within our budget" or "I leave it up to the finance team". Additionally, avoid using overly technical jargon or terminology that may confuse the interviewer.

"How do you measure success and set goals for both yourself and your team?"

Reason we ask: As an executive-level management candidate, we need to ensure that you have a clear understanding of how to measure success and set goals effectively for yourself and your team. Your answer should demonstrate your leadership and strategic thinking skills.

Example answer: "As a manager, I believe it is important to set clear, measurable goals for both myself and my team. I start by defining what success looks like for the team and then breaking down the larger goals into smaller, more achievable milestones. This not only helps to keep us on track but also motivates the team as they see their progress towards the end goal. I regularly check in with the team to ensure that everyone is on the same page and provide feedback to help them stay on track. Additionally, I measure success by regularly reviewing key performance indicators, such as revenue growth or customer satisfaction, to track progress and identify areas for improvement."

This answer demonstrates the candidate's understanding of the importance of setting clear goals and how to measure success through metrics. It also shows that the candidate values regular communication and feedback to ensure that everyone is aligned towards the same goals.

What to avoid: It is important to avoid vague or generic answers when responding to this question. Avoid answers that do not clearly demonstrate your understanding of how to set specific, measurable goals and track progress. Additionally, it is important to avoid answers that focus solely on individual performance rather than team performance. Remember to show that you are a collaborative leader who values the success of the team as a whole.

The Do's and Don'ts of Interviewing

There are a few key factors that can make or break your success in any interview process. To help you out, I've put together a list of these factors for you to review and keep in mind.

Things that you should do if you want to be more successful in your interviews.

Do thorough research before your interview.
To succeed in the interview, you need to prepare yourself by doing thorough research. Start by gathering as much information as possible about the company, their mission, and how the position you are interviewing for will contribute to achieving their goals. Additionally, familiarize yourself with the industry and who their main competitors are. To prepare for the specific job, study the job description, identify what qualities the ideal candidate should have, and think of ways to highlight your

strengths that align with those qualities. It is also beneficial to conduct social media research on the interviewers, as this can provide valuable insights into their background and interests. By learning about them, you can also prepare thoughtful questions to ask during the interview.

Prepare in advance.

Try to plan and prepare for your interview in advance so that you don't feel rushed or stressed out. It's essential to stay calm and relaxed in the hours leading up to your interview. Take some time to unwind and listen to something uplifting that puts you in a positive state of mind. Strive to be professional, but also friendly and approachable, as the hiring team will be evaluating your personality and attitude as well as your qualifications and experience.

Dress for the job you are interviewing for.

When preparing for your interview, consider the dress code for the job you want, and aim to dress at least one level above that standard. Remember, the version of you that the interviewer sees during the interview should be your best self. Dressing inappropriately, such as wearing jeans and a t-shirt to an interview for a business-casual job, shows a lack of understanding and interest in the position.

Focus on your accomplishments more than your duties.

As previously discussed in this book, the answers you provide during an interview hold a hierarchy of impressiveness. While a candidate may possess all the necessary skills for the job, providing weak answers can still leave a negative impression on the interviewer.

Include transferable skills if you are newly graduated or doing a career change.

If you do not have direct accomplishments or experience, use things that you have done that transfer well to the profile.

Express interest and enthusiasm for the opportunity.

A common mistake that candidates make is not being sure if they genuinely want the position, and this lack of commitment shows in their demeanor during the interview. If you are interviewing for a job, it is important to convey your interest in the position and make a positive impression. Ultimately, you want the decision to be yours to make. If you are offered the job and decide it is not the right career move, that is okay, as it will be your decision. However, if you come across as indifferent during the interview, the interviewer may decide that you are not the right fit for the job. Towards the end of the interview, show your interest by asking about the next steps and expressing what you like about the company and the opportunity.

Have good eye-contact and body language.

Showing lack of presence during an interview indicates a lack of interest, enthusiasm, and professionalism. This type of behavior can hinder your chances of being hired, as employers prefer candidates who show genuine interest and enthusiasm. Being disinterested and indifferent may suggest that you are only looking for a short-term position and not committed to doing high-quality work. So, it is crucial to stay engaged and present throughout the interview to make a positive impression.

Listen carefully to each question, even clarify what the interviewer is asking if needed.

Being mentally present during an interview is crucial for a candidate to succeed. It's common to get lost in your own thoughts and focus on what you're going to say next, but failing to pay attention to the interviewer's question can result in a poor answer. This not only reflects a lack of listening skills but also shows a lack of interest in the job and the interview process. To avoid this mistake, listen carefully to the question and take a moment to gather your thoughts before answering.

Answer all questions but use Answer/Ask.

The most impressive candidates are often those who exude a relaxed and confident demeanor during interviews. This book can help you achieve that. A candidate who engages in a back-and-forth conversation with the interviewer is more memorable than those who simply answer questions. When you ask questions, make sure they are relevant to the topic at hand. For example, if the interviewer asks about your preferred technology, you can answer and follow up by asking the interviewer about their preferences. Practice this technique of answering and then asking with someone beforehand and aim to use it about thirty percent of the time. This approach not only makes you stand out from other candidates, but it also helps you learn more about the job opportunity.

Example: Interviewer asks you *"What CRM software do you have experience with?"* and you respond with *"I have worked mostly with Salesforce, HubSpot, and Keap. What CRM do you use here and how do you like it?"*

Practice before your interview.

Rather than memorizing your answers, practice articulating your main points confidently. A helpful technique is recording yourself leaving your answers in your own voicemail and then listening to them later for self-reflection. Alternatively, consider finding a friend or colleague to conduct "mock interviews" with you. One effective exercise is to play the role of the interviewer and ask questions based on the ideal candidate profile to determine whether they would be a good fit. Through this process, you can gain valuable insights into areas you need to improve upon in your own answers.

Send a thank you email or note after every interview.

Sending a thank you note after your interview is a great way to show your appreciation and leave a positive impression. It is recommended to send the thank you note within 24 hours of the interview or one day before the interviewer makes their decision if they have specified a date. An email is usually the best way to send the note, but if the industry is more personal, a physical note may be more appropriate. If you do not have the interviewer's email, you can send it to the recruiter and ask them to forward it to the interviewer on your behalf.

Follow-up thank you email/notes should be short, typically 3-4 sentences long and should include:

1. Thank the interviewer for their time.

2. Remind them of the top 1 or 2 things about your fit for the job that you believe impressed them.

3. If needed, try to mitigate any concerns about your fit with the job that they expressed. (One sentence.)

4. Convey interest in moving forward with the interview process or receiving an offer for the job.

Accept that this is a process, and you will not get every job that you want.

Perseverance is key in the job interview process. Even if you have a less than perfect interview, it is important to stay positive and learn from your mistakes. Take an honest look at your performance and make small adjustments to improve your approach. It can be challenging, but keeping a positive attitude is essential for success.

I recall working with a recent college graduate who had no professional experience, but was determined to become a pharmaceutical sales representative. She had some social awkwardness but was likable and eager to learn. While she was not a top candidate, I believed in her and arranged for her to interview with two of my clients. Despite not receiving an offer, she persevered and continued to interview on her own. Eventually, she landed a job with a major company and has spent over two decades in her desired career. With each interview, she gained more confidence and improved her approach.

Remember to stay persistent, remain positive, and keep working at it. Even if you face rejection or setbacks, every interview is a learning opportunity to help you become a better candidate.

Things that you should avoid if you want to be more successful in your interviews:

Forgetting something.

Allow yourself ample time to prepare for your interview. This will help you avoid any last-minute mishaps and ensure that you do not forget anything important. Before your interview, the hiring manager may request that you review specific information, complete a questionnaire, or undertake an assignment. Make sure you have completed all these tasks before your interview. It is important to double- and triple-check everything to ensure you don't miss anything important.

Arriving late.

When it comes to face-to-face interviews, it's best to arrive at the location ten to fifteen minutes before your scheduled interview time. However, for phone or video interviews, make sure to be ready three to five minutes before the scheduled time, whether it's logging in to a video platform or having your phone nearby and fully charged.

No call/no show.

Failing to show up for your interview without any notice, especially through a phone call, is a surefire way to miss out on a job opportunity. It can have a long-lasting negative impact on your reputation, not only for the job in question but also for future opportunities. This kind of behavior is unprofessional and can lead to a lasting negative impression, which may harm your chances of securing the position you desire."

Sounding as though your answers are just rehearsed words you think you are supposed to say.

Although it is important to prepare for expected interview questions, it is equally important to avoid appearing too rehearsed. Instead of memorizing responses word-for-word, focus on bullet points you want to cover in your answers.

Practicing ahead of time is helpful, but try to strike a balance between preparedness and spontaneity. Being sincere and relaxed during the interview will go a long way in impressing your interviewer.

Leave your phone volume on during the interview.

Although it may seem like a small detail, forgetting to silence your phone during an interview can have a negative impact on your candidacy. While it may not be a dealbreaker, it could make a difference if another candidate is equally qualified. It may come across as unprofessional and suggest that you lack attention to detail. Therefore, make sure to double-check that your phone is silenced before the interview to avoid any potential distractions or interruptions.

Speaking negatively about previous jobs.

When interviewing for a job, it's important to maintain a positive attitude and avoid speaking negatively about previous employers or colleagues. Complaining or gossiping may lead the interviewer to perceive you as a toxic ex-employee. Instead, focus on your accomplishments, objectives, and connections. If asked about a bad experience, frame it as a learning opportunity. Highlight your interest in the new company and how your skills and experiences align with their goals. This positive approach will make you a more attractive candidate and increase your chances of success.

Being arrogant or rude to anyone.

It's crucial to be courteous and friendly to everyone you encounter while interviewing at a company. Remember, the interviewer might ask for feedback from any staff member you interacted with during your visit. Therefore, it's crucial to be polite and kind to all employees, from the receptionist to the janitor. It's also an excellent opportunity to demonstrate your interpersonal skills, as being pleasant and engaging with people you meet can give the interviewer a positive impression of you.

Being dishonest.

Lying or even appearing dishonest can be an automatic dealbreaker, even if you have all the qualifications. Employers have ways of verifying information, and if they find out you've lied, it's game over. Even if you somehow manage to get hired, any dishonesty that is later uncovered can lead to termination. It's always better to be honest, even if it means admitting a weakness or a lack of experience in a certain area.

Delay in responding to recruiters or hiring managers.

Feedback is crucial after an interview with someone besides the recruiter. Hiring managers and recruiters may also request clarification on something you mentioned during an interview. Failing to provide timely responses or withholding information gives the impression that you are not motivated to get the job. It is important to provide requested information promptly and with transparency.

Over-explaining.

When answering interview questions, it's important to be concise and to the point. A good rule of thumb is to keep your responses to about thirty to sixty seconds. If your answer goes over ninety seconds, it may be too long and lose the interviewer's attention. Try to avoid meandering or rambling answers. If the interviewer wants more detail or clarification, they will ask follow-up questions. Remember to be concise and clear while still answering the question that is being asked.

Giving vague answers.

When answering interview questions, make sure to provide specific examples to support your responses. Vague answers can come across as evasive, and can give the impression that you are trying to hide something or are not being truthful. Remember, the interviewer is trying to assess your skills and experience, so providing concrete examples helps to demonstrate your qualifications and build credibility. Avoid giving general or overly broad responses, and instead provide details that highlight your strengths and accomplishments.

Demonstrating a lack of taking responsibility.

When discussing past mistakes, avoid blaming others. During an interview, you may be asked to talk about a time when you made a mistake at work. It's important to take ownership of your actions and avoid placing the blame solely on your colleagues. Claiming that you've never made a mistake may come across as insincere. Instead, talk about what you learned from the mistake and how you would handle the situation differently if it were to happen again.

Don't get the most out of your time.

It's important to remember that interviews are not just about answering questions but also about asking them. If you only focus on answering questions and do not ask any, it can leave a negative impression on the interviewer. Research the company beforehand and prepare a list of questions to ask. Use these to guide you during the interview, or when it feels appropriate to use the Answer/Ask technique. Most interviewers will leave time at the end of the interview for you to ask questions, so be sure to take advantage of this opportunity. Asking good questions demonstrates your interest in the job and can give you an advantage over other candidates. For more information on the best questions to ask, check out the chapter titled 'Best Questions That Candidates Ask the Interviewer'.

Being unprofessional.

It's essential to maintain proper posture during the interview and avoid fidgeting with your hands or feet or any items around you. An interviewer once shared with me a story about a candidate who put their feet up on a chair during the interview, and another who was chewing gum. While these may seem like minor issues, they can create a negative impression. Keep in mind that during an interview, you are expected to be at your best, and anything less may lead the interviewer to wonder how you might behave as an employee. To avoid such mishaps, it's best to maintain a professional demeanor throughout the interview process.

Give a bad impression of your personality.

When interviewing for a job, be aware that certain personality traits may lead the interviewer to screen you out of the hiring process. Although interviewers do not explicitly test you for these traits, their experience in hiring informs them on how these traits can lead to problematic hires. These traits come up in discussions with hiring managers and impact the decision-making process. This is especially true for startups where smaller teams require employees to work closely with each other. While you cannot change your personality, it is important to be self-aware and avoid projecting these traits.

Top personality traits that interviewers watch out for.

1. Overly self-absorbed.
2. Dishonest/untrustworthy.
3. Inability to take responsibility for mistakes, especially by blaming others.
4. Inflexible and not open to new ideas, suggestions, or coaching. (I would include the "know-it-all" candidates in this category.)
5. Fragile ego that is unable to process constructive criticism.
6. Reckless risk taking. (Calculated risk taking is great, but careless actions are not.)
7. Bitter/angry or anything else that might indicate a future toxic co-worker/employee.

It's essential to treat every interaction with any company employee as a type of interview. Candidates might perform well in the interview with the hiring manager but fail to get the job because of a negative impression from the receptionist or anyone else they interact with. It's also important to keep up your professional demeanor in every meeting or conversation, even if it's a casual one. A moment of letting your guard down and saying something inappropriate can jeopardize your chances of getting hired. Always remember that every interaction is a chance to make a positive impression and be considered for the position.

How to Stand Out from Others

The employer's selection process is like a funnel, with numerous candidates entering at the top, and fewer progressing through each stage. As you move through the process, the company evaluates you and your competition, gathering feedback from everyone who interviews you. To be the candidate offered the job, you need to make a lasting impression from the very beginning.

Start by gaining a deep understanding of the position beyond what's in the job ad. Knowing what makes an ideal hire for the role will help you stand out. Reach out to your professional network for insights on the personality traits and skills that are successful in the position. Additionally, research the company, department, and interviewer to get a better sense of what they are looking for in a candidate.

During the interview, try to establish a personal connection with the interviewer. If you have any similarities with them, such as a shared background or interest, use that to your advantage. Be natural and relatable, and don't forget to use their name when speaking or sending an email. Take note of the names of those you meet and refer to them in the future.

Remember, your dream job is also someone else's dream. To stand out, you must do the small things that create a positive memory of your interactions with the company and its employees.

Here are a few things that will help you stand out.

Be fully prepared.
Before your interview, it is crucial to do your research on the company, its history, strategy, and executives. Take note of any information you can gather about the individuals who will be conducting your interviews. This pre-interview preparation will have a significant impact on the actual interview, and will help you establish a connection with the interviewer. The more you know about the company, the more comfortable you will feel answering their questions and the more insightful your questions

will be. Use this knowledge to your advantage during the interview and show the interviewer that you are invested in the company and the position.

Keep in mind that your interview will begin as soon as you arrive at the organization.

During job interviews, many companies request feedback from their front desk staff on the applicant's attitude. To present yourself as organized and professional, make sure you have the name of your interviewer and the time of your appointment. Practice polite and professional behavior, including your tone and body language. Remember that as soon as you step inside the building, you are in interview mode and should conduct yourself accordingly.

Unique Value Proposition (UVP).

Crafting a UVP is a powerful tool to establish your personal candidate brand during an interview. It is a concise version of your response to the "Tell me about yourself" question, highlighting your top skills and attributes that overlap with the ideal profile. Your statement should be no longer than thirty seconds, or three to four sentences. This statement can serve as an introduction at job fairs or networking events, or as a way to start a conversation during an interview. You can also use it to support your other answers by providing examples of your skills. For more guidance on crafting an effective UVP statement, refer to the companion workbook.

Be a good listener and answer the questions asked of you.

It may seem obvious, but many candidates start formulating their answer before the interviewer has finished asking the question. This can cause them to miss important details and leave out parts of their answer, giving the impression that they are not good listeners. If you don't listen carefully during the interview, the employer may assume that you will not follow directions or take feedback well on the job. Therefore, it is important to listen carefully to each question and make sure that you fully understand it before providing an answer.

Answer/Ask.

The majority of interviews are structured in a one-sided way where the interviewer asks the questions, and the candidate responds. However, the most impressive candidates are not only able to provide answers but also engage in a professional conversation with the interviewer. This Answer/Ask technique was previously mentioned in the chapter on The Dos and Don'ts of Interviewing. While it may require practice, it can be very effective when executed properly. It should not come across as forced or interrupt the interviewer, but rather should be a natural back-and-forth exchange. A follow-up question can be asked about thirty percent of the time after answering a question, which demonstrates confidence and engagement.

Example: If you are a business analyst and are asked about which ERP systems you have worked with at your last job, answer the question, and then ask something about their ERP system; which system do they use, which version, how long have they used it, how does the interviewer like it? Do not let the interview go too far off-course, but a natural back and forth will make you stand out in a positive way.

Forgive yourself if you make a mistake in the process.
Mistakes happen during interviews, but how you react to them can make all the difference. It's an opportunity to demonstrate resilience and composure in the face of adversity. It is essential to focus on the moment and not allow a mistake to ruin the rest of the meeting. Acknowledge the error, but quickly pivot back to the current question as if it were the first. Interviewers will remember how you handle the situation and your ability to recover more

than the mistake itself. This is a chance to show your ability to handle setbacks professionally and with confidence.

Pay attention to the little things.

Small things often make a big impact when it comes to building a positive impression of yourself as a job candidate. Arrive ten to fifteen minutes early for any in-person interview to demonstrate your punctuality and reliability. If you are going to be late, be sure to communicate with the recruiter or hiring manager in advance. Sending thank-you emails or notes after your interviews is also an important detail that many candidates overlook. While these may seem like simple gestures, they can make all the difference in setting you apart from other applicants who do not take the time to do them.

Closing statement.

When ending an interview, it is crucial to leave a lasting impression on the interviewer. Make sure to express gratitude for their time, convey that you enjoyed meeting them, show interest in the next steps of the process, and give a brief summary of what makes you a good fit for the role.

It's essential to be genuine and specific with your answers. Avoid using rehearsed or monotone responses, as this may cause you to fade into the background or be easily forgotten. Additionally, refrain from over-exaggerating your skills and abilities.

Ultimately, what sets a candidate apart is their unique characteristics and attributes that can benefit the manager and the company. By following the advice in this chapter, you can impress the interviewer and showcase the skills and traits that make you stand out from other candidates.

M. L. Miller

146

Best Questions That Candidates Ask the Interviewer

As you near the end of your interview, you will likely be asked if you have any questions for the interviewer. This is a crucial opportunity to gain insights into whether the job is a good fit for your goals, showcase your suitability for the position, and refine your understanding of the ideal profile. Failing to ask questions gives the impression that you are not a serious candidate or are simply seeking any job at the moment.

To make a positive impression, you should ask insightful questions of your interviewers. You can incorporate questions throughout the interview using the Answer/Ask technique mentioned earlier. When asked about remaining questions, ask two or three of the most relevant ones. I have listed some of the best questions from candidates that I have heard below. Before your interview, compile a list of the most relevant seven to ten questions you like. This way, you will still have two or three at the end that were left unanswered. You can even save questions on your phone or on a piece of paper and refer to them during the interview.

(Quick note that most companies will be the ones to bring up compensation. DO NOT ask about compensation at the beginning of an interview process, it shows that your priorities are wrong.)

I have broken down the best questions into four categories:

About the interviewer.

"What was your background before being hired here? How has that benefited you?"

"What do you love most about working here?"

"How would you describe your own management style?"

"What do you enjoy doing outside of work?"

"Is this the career path that you envisioned for yourself when you got your start?"

"What do you wish you knew back when you were in my shoes?"

"Why did you decide to work here?"

Company culture.

"How would you describe the company culture here?"

"What type of employee has been most successful here?"

"What about an employee that did not work out here, why didn't they succeed?"

"What are new employees most surprised by in their first few months here?"

"Why do employees love to work here?"

"What type of hires do not last long with your company?"

Interest in being successful with the company.

"What would you need me to focus on in the first month on the job?"

"What additional responsibilities can be gained over time in this role?"

"What has been the biggest challenge for this role?"

"What are the biggest company goals for the next few years, and how does this position affect those goals?"

"What have people who reported to you in the past done to be successful?"

"What would I need to accomplish in the first year in this job for you to view me as a successful hire?"

"What do you want this role to accomplish in the first 90 days?"

"How do you measure success for the person in this role?"

"What advice would you give to the person you hire in order for them to be successful in this role?"

"What have past employees done to become successful in this type of role here?"

"What are the biggest challenges that the company faces, and how can I help in this role?"

"Who is the company's biggest competitor, and what can I do in this role to help beat them?"

"What is the one trait that you have seen in people who have been very successful in this type of role?"

Due diligence.

"How would you explain this job in your own words?"

"What about my background made you choose me for the interview?"

"What does the interview process look like?"

"Why is the position available?"

"How long has this position been open?"

(If it has already been a couple of months or longer, here is a follow-up: *"What seems to be missing from candidates you have interviewed so far?"*)

"What is your timeframe for hiring someone for this position?"

"What do you think the company's biggest accomplishments will be in the next few years?"

Closing for the offer.

"What skills or experience do you wish I had to make myself a better fit for this position?"

"What are the next steps in the process?"

"What can I clarify about my background to show you that I am the best fit for the job?"

"When would you need me to start?"

(Subtle way to get them to picture hiring you)

"Is there anything in my skills or experience that you feel I am lacking compared to what you are looking for?"

When it comes to the interview process, it's essential to remember that the interviewers will discuss their impressions and recommendations about each candidate throughout and at the end of the process. The questions that you ask or don't ask can significantly impact their decision-making. So, it's crucial to take the time to get it right.

Never say that you have no questions when asked. Use the information gained from your conversation to make any necessary changes for your next interview. Remember to be aware of the time and respect any indications that the interview is coming to a close. Avoid asking questions if the interviewer is running late, as this may cause them to become impatient and leave a negative impression about you.

Employer Red Flags

Preparing for an interview can help you become a stronger and more confident candidate. But it's important to remember that the interview is not just about demonstrating why you're the best match for the job. You are also evaluating the company to see if it's a good fit for you.

One way to approach interviewing is to compare it to dating. Like people looking for a romantic partner, employers have an ideal profile of what they want in an employee. They are not trying to determine if you're a good or bad person, but if you're a good fit for what they need.

Just like in dating, a one-sided evaluation process isn't ideal. You have your own idea of what you're looking for in a job and it's important to pay attention to any red flags that may arise during the interview process. Don't be fooled by false positive impressions that could lead to a bad or toxic work situation.

By being aware of what you're looking for and paying attention to any warning signs, you can approach the interview process with more confidence and increase your chances of finding a good match for both you and the company.

Here are employer red flags for you to be extremely cautious of.

Asking you illegal interview questions.

The legality of questions that employers are allowed to ask varies by country and state. It is important to research and understand what can and cannot be asked where you and the employer are located. For example, in the United States, questions regarding age, religion, race, national origin, gender, marital status, pregnancy, or disability are not allowed. In some states, questions about current compensation are also prohibited. However, you can be asked if your age meets a legal requirement for the job, if you are authorized to work in the country, and if you can physically perform the job duties.

If you are asked a question that you believe is prohibited, it is not recommended to be confrontational. Try to answer the question without providing protected information. If the interviewer persists or there is a pattern of illegal questions, politely end the interview and leave. Most countries have a government agency to report such incidents if necessary. It is important to pay attention to red flags, as asking illegal questions can indicate what kind of employer they will be.

High employee turnover compared to other companies in the same industry.

While some employers may experience temporary high employee turnover due to changes in management or strategy, it is important to be cautious of those with a history of frequent turnover. Even if the opportunity seems promising on paper, take the time to understand the reasons behind their high turnover rate.

To gather more information, you can research the company on LinkedIn and compare the number of current employees to previous employees. Additionally, look at the length of time current employees have been with the company. If many employees have been there for less than a year, it could indicate rapid expansion or high turnover. It is crucial to thoroughly evaluate any potential employer to avoid finding yourself in a work environment with a history of instability and turnover.

The description of the job in the interview does not match the description in the ad / or is very unclear.

When an employer describes a different job or is unclear about what the position entails during the interview, it could be a classic bait-and-switch tactic. Employers use this tactic when they realize that the job isn't that attractive. If the job description they give you during the interview is different from what was advertised, it's essential to question a few things. If they change the job description once, will they do it again in the future? How bad is the job if they cannot provide a clear description of it?

Negative atmosphere.

Observing the behavior of employees in a company can give you a good idea of the work environment. Pay close attention to the interaction between co-workers, especially if you are on-site for an interview. Take note of how many employees seem to like each other and appear to be happy working together. If the employees, who are the ones that know the company's work culture best, do not seem content or satisfied, then you should consider that it could be you in the near future. So, be attentive to how the employees behave and interact, as it can be an important factor in deciding whether or not to pursue a job opportunity at the company.

Disrespectful of your time.

When interviewing for a job, it is common courtesy for both the interviewer and the interviewee to respect each other's time. However, there are times when a delay or an unforeseen event may cause the interviewer to be late. In such situations, the interviewer should be apologetic and respectful towards the candidate, who had to wait. This is a red flag that should not be ignored. If the interviewer does not respect your time during the interview process, it is unlikely that they will respect you once you become an employee. While there is no need to be impolite, this behavior should warn you about the kind of culture you may be working in if you accept the job.

Compensation does not match expectations.

When it comes to discussing compensation during the interview process, some companies will disclose the range at the beginning, while others will bring it up at the end. It is crucial to do your research beforehand and have a good understanding of the market value for your position, level of experience, and education. If a company appears to have champagne tastes on a beer budget, be cautious, as it may indicate a culture of expecting more from their employees than they are willing to pay for. However, there are exceptions, such as jobs where gaining experience is the greatest value or startups that may offer equity in the company as compensation. Remember to consider all aspects of the compensation package, including benefits and growth opportunities, when evaluating an offer.

They are asking you to complete free work as part of the interview process.

If a company asks you to complete unpaid work that is part of their regular business, it is a big red flag. Many interview processes include steps where you may be asked to complete a hypothetical exercise as an evaluation tool to test your skill level. However, asking candidates to do work for free is unacceptable, and it should be a warning sign. If their culture permits them to exploit job candidates, then how do you think they are going to treat you as an employee?

Negative company reviews.

Before you go in for an interview, make sure to research reviews online and within your professional network from former employees of the company. Keep in mind that disgruntled former employees may have a bias when writing those reviews, so use it more as a guide to things you should question rather than unimpeachable facts. Look for patterns where the same negative comments are made by multiple former employees. These patterns should be red flags, especially if they relate to your main concerns about the job or company.

During your interview process, pay attention to things you see or hear that match what the negative reviews claim. Take the opportunity to ask questions about any concerns you may have in a respectful and professional manner. This will not only help you to better understand the company's culture and practices, but it will also show the interviewer that you are proactive and engaged in the process.

You are asked about how you have dealt with working with difficult people.

If you hear variations of the question 'Can you deal with difficult people?' multiple times during your interview process, it might be a warning sign of a negative or toxic work environment. Although hearing this question once in an interview is not necessarily a red flag, it is still important to ask follow-up questions to gain a better understanding of the role and the people you may be working with. When answering this question, use the Answer/Ask technique to gather more information. If you get a negative answer, be aware that it could be a sign of difficult co-workers. Be cautious of phrases like 'they have high standards,' 'they're a perfectionist,' or 'they take some getting used to.' These statements could be a warning of a challenging work environment.

They gossip about previous employees.

A toxic workplace can cause a lot of problems, so it is important to avoid them. Gossip is one of the most toxic behaviors that can exist in a workplace, and if an interviewer engages in this behavior during an interview, it is a sign that the company has a toxic culture. If they are willing to smear a former employee's reputation to make themselves look better to you, they will likely do the same thing to you in the future. This is a huge red flag, and you should proceed with caution.

Like dating, the interview process is about finding a good match between employer and employee. Confident and likable people tend to do better in both. It is important to confidently present yourself as a good fit for the job, but also evaluate the employer to see if it is a good fit for you. Ignoring red flags during the evaluation stage can lead to regret later on. Keep presenting yourself as a good match, but continue to ask legitimate questions professionally during the interview process. A good employer will see this as a sign that you are serious about a long-term working relationship.

What to Expect from Different Interview Processes

Employers adopt diverse interview formats, and candidates may feel bewildered and distracted when they encounter a format that they did not anticipate. To assist you in navigating through these different interview types, I have compiled a list below, providing details on each one. This will help you become familiar with them, instill confidence, and allow you to remain focused on your objective should you ever encounter them.

Interview formats.

1-on-1.

The one-on-one interview is the most familiar type for job seekers. During this interview, you and the interviewer will have a discussion about your background and the opportunity. The majority of the advice in this book can be directly applied to this type of interview.

1-on-1 sequential.

A series of one-on-one interviews constitutes the sequential interviewing process, where you progress to the next round of interviews if you perform well. Most people are familiar with this format, but it is worth noting that these processes usually culminate in a final interview, which may use one of the other interview formats.

Panel.

The panel interview can be an intimidating experience for candidates. This type of interview involves one candidate meeting with two or more interviewers at the same time. Typically, there are between three to five interviewers on a panel. Employers conduct panel interviews to expedite the hiring process, make collaborative hiring decisions based on seeing and hearing the same things, and train new interviewers. To succeed in a panel interview, it is crucial to remain calm and confident, and avoid focusing solely on one interviewer. Instead, make good eye contact with everyone on the panel, spending slightly more time with the interviewer who asked the question. After the interview, all the interviewers will provide feedback on your suitability for the role, so it is essential to create as many advocates on the panel as possible.

Half/full day.

The half/full day of interviewing format is typically reserved for the final stage of an interview process, as it allows multiple stakeholders to participate in the hiring decision. During this type of interview, you will typically meet with your potential manager, peers, human resources representatives, managers from other teams or departments, and the hiring manager's boss. It is essential to maintain your energy and enthusiasm throughout the day, as this format can be long and arduous. Pay attention to staying hydrated and eating or snacking as needed. It is worth noting that I once had a great candidate perform exceptionally well in the morning interviews, only to perform poorly in the afternoon due to a lack of energy. As a result, they were not hired. Therefore, be mindful of your energy level and enthusiasm in each interview to maximize your chances of success.

Informal.

An informal interview is often used for senior positions, such as taking a candidate to lunch or dinner. However, it can also be as simple as having a peer give you a tour of the facility or chatting with you in the lobby. One common mistake that candidates make during informal interviews is letting their guard down and forgetting that they are still being evaluated. It is crucial to remain relaxed yet professional, positive, and focused on demonstrating how you fit the ideal profile for the position. So, while you should strive to be as comfortable as possible during informal interviews, remember that it is still a part of the interview process.

Phone.

While an initial phone screen is typically a part of most interview processes, it can be included at any point along the way. One of the great advantages of conducting an interview over the phone is that the interviewer cannot see you, which allows you to have your notes, resume, job description, and profile in front of you during the interview. It may seem insignificant, but standing and smiling when you speak on the phone can create a more positive impression. Smiling will make your voice project more confidently and warmly. After the call (or video call) ends, take a few moments to jot down notes while the conversation is still fresh in your memory. Record any comments the interviewer made that provide more insight into the job duties, company culture, or any other information that can give you an advantage in future interviews.

Video.

Video interviews are becoming increasingly common and have presented a learning curve for some candidates. These interviews take place over video conferencing platforms such as Zoom, MS Teams, Google Meet, Skype, or similar platforms. I have seen some candidates turn off their cameras and only use audio during the interview. It is crucial to treat a video interview like an in-person meeting by dressing professionally and always keeping your camera turned on unless you have a technical issue. Many video conferencing platforms offer virtual backgrounds, which can be used if your physical background is distracting. I have also experienced interviews where the candidate's camera was placed to the side of their computer screen, making it appear as though they were not making eye contact. Before any video interview, make sure to test your camera and audio, and position the camera in a way that allows you to give the impression of making eye contact with the interviewer.

One-way video application.

Some companies have begun using pre-recorded video answers to screening questions as part of the application process. In addition to the advice that I gave for video interviews, you should uncover the details of the settings for your video application. Some will allow you to record a video as many times as you want before submitting, while others will have a limit. With formats that limit the times that you can record, you can practice your answers using your smartphone before recording in the application itself.

Peer.

Interviews conducted by potential future co-workers can occur in a formal 1-on-1, panel, video, or casual setting. Such interviews provide a unique perspective and offer insights that may not be available through other interview formats. However, these interviews are also riddled with potential pitfalls. Some candidates may feel overly relaxed when speaking with a peer, which may result in giving negative responses or asking inappropriate questions that they would not ask the hiring manager. To succeed in your interview process, it is essential to remember that you are always being interviewed, and the peer will likely be asked about their interaction with you. So, always maintain a professional demeanor, regardless of who you are speaking to during the interview process.

Stress.

If you are interviewing for a job that will require you to deal with stressful situations, then it is a good idea for the employer to find out how you handle yourself under stress. When I have used this technique, I typically change my tone of voice and act more aggressively towards the candidate, but stress interviews can take on different forms. At the very least you should expect to be asked uncomfortable or stressful questions that are meant to emulate the type of stress in this job. The most successful way to prepare for this type of interview is to do enough research to know whether to expect one. Being surprised by these types of interviews increases the chances of failure. If you do recognize that you are being tested on how you handle stress, try to think about the ideal profile they are trying to hire and do what you can to demonstrate how you would respond if hired. When you are researching the company, do a search with the company name and "Stress Interview" to see if this is something you should expect.

Group.

Group interviews involve a group of candidates meeting with one or a few interviewers at once. While I am not a big fan of this type of interview, its primary purpose is to quickly eliminate candidates. The interviewer will gather several candidates and give a presentation about the job opportunity, which may not be the most attractive job available on the market. Candidates not interested in the position will be instructed to leave, and the interviewer will continue with the remaining candidates. There is not much advice I can offer to perform well in this type of interview as it is more about determining whether the job aligns with your interests. However, ensure that you ask questions and comprehend the role. The reason many employers use a group interview format is that numerous candidates have previously declined the job offer. As such, you should question why this is the case and decide accordingly. . . . .

The Job Offer

After successfully completing the interview process, you may have an offer of employment coming your way. Although companies typically make verbal offers, most will follow up with a written offer letter. Your offer will likely have an expiration date since employers need to move on to the next candidate if you decline the offer. One week is the standard time frame, and while you can negotiate the deadline, asking for two or more weeks may suggest that the offer is not your top choice.

While most candidates do not negotiate job offers, those who do tend to earn more money. Negotiating the details of a job offer is more successful if you have followed the advice in this book and created a high-value candidate image with the company. The most crucial piece of advice is that you should negotiate your job offer in most cases. Conduct research to increase your chances of success.

Salary is not the only aspect you can negotiate. Depending on the company, you can request better shifts, company equity, education or training reimbursement, more responsibilities to gain experience, and other benefits.

For more information on successful salary negotiation, please read *SoaringME.com Guide to Successful Salary Negotiation*. However, be cautious when seeking other advice, as I have seen poor advice given by unqualified individuals.

When asked about your salary expectations, avoid staying silent as some suggest. Playing negotiation games may work in some limited cases, but it is not always effective. If an employer wants to hire you, they may overlook any concerns they have about your behavior. However, most of the time, playing negotiation games may make you appear untrustworthy or misguided. Instead, prepare to answer the question about your salary expectations professionally and know what a fair and realistic market price is for your services.

If you found this book to be valuable, please remember to leave a rating to let others know.

Visit SoaringME.com or ask your favorite bookstore for our other books to help your career.

About the Author

M.L. Miller was born in Washington state, grew up in Oregon and, having lived in various places around the United States, he is now back living in the Pacific Northwest with his wife, Wilawan.

Having studied Economics/Finance at the University of Hartford in Connecticut, M.L. began a career in recruitment in 1997, working for hundreds of client companies from Fortune 100 large companies to start-ups. During this time, he has conducted somewhere between twenty and thirty thousand job interviews and has hired thousands of employees in a variety of roles from entry-level positions to C-Suite and Board-Level. During his career he managed a corporate recruiting team, increasing their hires by over 33% in under two years. He started Ethical Recruiters, Inc., an executive recruitment firm and later SoaringME, a company that educates candidates on how to be more successful in job interviewing.

Within this framework, M.L. has also published several books related to the subject:

· *SoaringME The Ultimate Guide to Successful Job Searching.*

· *SoaringME The Ultimate Guide to Successful Job Interviewing.*

· *SoaringME COMPANION WORKBOOK The Ultimate Guide to Successful Job Interviewing.*

· *SoaringME.com: Guide to Successful Salary Negotiation.*

He also has several Ultimate Guides on interviewing for specific careers.

In his free time, M.L. is an avid cyclist and has ridden the annual 200-mile Seattle-to-Portland bike ride five times so far. He also enjoys traveling domestically and internationally.

M.L. has worked with homeless military veterans for a couple of years through a non-profit organization. He used his experience to help them improve interviewing skills, write resumes, and obtain employment to get back on their feet. He also raises money for children's mental health charities.

In the future, M.L. plans to continue his career in talent acquisition. His personal goal is to one day combine his love of cycling and travel to complete 100-mile bike rides on five different continents.

His favorite quote is "Every strike brings me closer to the next home run..." – Babe Ruth.